# EVERYDAY DEATH

ALSO BY ANN JONES

*Uncle Tom's Campus*
*Women Who Kill*

# EVERYDAY DEATH

## THE CASE OF BERNADETTE POWELL

## ANN JONES

HOLT, RINEHART AND WINSTON
NEW YORK

Published by Holt, Rinehart and Winston,
383 Madison Avenue, New York, New York 10017.
Published simultaneously in Canada by Holt, Rinehart and
Winston of Canada, Limited.

Library of Congress Cataloging in Publication Data
Jones, Ann, 1937–
Everyday death.
1. Powell, Bernadette, 1952–      —Trials, litigation,
etc.    2. Trials (Murder)—New York (State)—Ithaca.
3. Abused wives—New York (State)    I. Title.
KF224.P63J66    1985        345.73'02523        84-22547
                            347.3052523
ISBN 0-03-062976-4


Designed by Susan Hood
Printed in the United States of America
10   9   8   7   6   5   4   3   2

Permission to quote from *Daybook: The Journal of an Artist*
© 1982 by Anne Truitt has been granted by Pantheon Books, a
Division of Random House, Inc.

ISBN 0-03-062976-4

For Meg

*Unless we are very, very careful, we doom each other by holding onto images of one another based on preconceptions that are in turn based on indifference to what is other than ourselves. This indifference can be, in its extreme, a form of murder and seems to me a rather common phenomenon.*

—Anne Truitt, DAYBOOK: THE JOURNAL
OF AN ARTIST


*Justice is like the kingdom of God—it is not without us as a fact, it is within us as a great yearning.*

—George Eliot, ROMOLA

# CONTENTS

# ACKNOWLEDGMENTS

Many people helped me look into this case and write this book. They know who they are and how valuable their help was to me, and most of them would just as soon leave it at that. But I am particularly indebted to some who shared with me their special skills and long experience. Townsend "Bud" Ackerman taught me a lot about how to investigate; and Rebecca Allerton, working as my research assistant, patiently helped me to do it. Dr. Robert E. Gould, Professor of Psychiatry at New York Medical College, advised me on psychiatric matters; and Martin Stolar, Bernadette Powell's attorney, explained the law and cooperated in my research without attempting to guide my conclusions. Superintendent Janice Cummings of Albion Correctional Facility made possible my long interviews with Bernadette Powell when Powell was imprisoned there; and Superintendent Elaine Lord of Bedford Hills Correctional Facility acquainted me with that prison where Powell is now incarcerated.

I am grateful to those friends who read and criticized the manuscript: William Zinsser, who read a troublesome chapter, and especially Ann-Ellen Lesser, who with extraordinary grace edited the whole text more than once. And I am grateful to those who took me in: the Writers Room in New York City and the MacDowell Colony, where I wrote parts of this book, and the Millay Colony for the Arts, where I finished it. That it was finished at all is due largely to the encouragement of my great friend and literary agent Frances Goldin, my past and present editors Gladys Topkis, Jennifer Josephy, and Richard Seaver, and my writer-friends—Joan Silber, Susan Brownmiller, Norma Millay, Lois Gould, Nancy Milford, Angeline Goreau, and Dan Domench—who, by their brave example and unremitting human kindness, keep me keeping on.

My greatest debt, of course, is to Bernadette Powell, who granted me access to every record of her life and confided in me more than I would have thought to ask. At the heart of my story about her is *her* story, and I could not have told my version of it if she had not so bravely told her version of it to me. In return for this unflagging cooperation she asked of me only that I tell the truth, as I saw it, and that I be, as she was, both loving and diligent.

# AUTHOR'S NOTE

The characters in this factual story are identified by their real names. One of the curious and confusing features of this case is how many of those names are the same. There are three Smiths, all unrelated: Herman Smith, the homicide victim; Al Smith, the prosecution's star witness; and Allen G. Smith, a Senior Investigator with the New York State Police. There are three Browns, also unrelated to one another: David Brown, an acquaintance of Powell's and Dorlyn Brown, a motel employee, both witnesses for the prosecution; and Ralph Brown who was one of Powell's first friends in Ithaca and did not give evidence at the trial. There are two Thomases: Anthony (Tony), a witness for the prosecution, and his brother Michael, a witness for the defense. There are two Oscar Lee Powells, Senior and Junior, Bernadette's father and brother. And there are two women named Diane Nelson.

The documents quoted—police and court records, newspaper accounts, and letters—are reproduced exactly, their spelling and grammar unrepaired.

# EVERYDAY DEATH

# INTRODUCTION

I met Bernadette Powell in March 1979 in the women's lavatory on the second floor of the Tompkins County Courthouse in Ithaca, New York. She was on trial for her life. For several days, sitting behind her in the courtroom, I watched her straight back, the way she never slumped or wilted, the way she occasionally leaned sideways to whisper to her attorney, her body still rigid. Whenever the judge called a recess, she rose, still straight-backed as a ballerina, turned from the bench, and walked steadily in her sensible shoes up the aisle past the spectators and through the swinging door at the back of the courtroom. At the same time a slight, poker-faced young woman—whom the other reporters in the press row identified as Rebecca Allerton, head of the local Tompkins County Task Force on Battered Women— rose from the front row to my right and followed Powell out of the room.

One day I followed, too—out the swinging door and into the next door on my left, the women's room. It was a tiny room, and Powell leaned against the washbasin, huddled into the corner behind the door like some crumpled rag doll. In the courtroom she was all hard edges and starch, but here, out of sight, she was limp and so diminished that at first I didn't see her. I introduced myself to Allerton. "I'd like very much to talk to Ms. Powell," I said, and at once

*1*

a hand appeared on Allerton's shoulder, pushing her aside. "You want to talk to me?" Powell snapped. "I'll talk to you. What do you want to know? You want to see my scars? Just look at that. Why don't you write about that?"

She tugged up the sleeves of her jersey and thrust her hands into my face, turning the underside of her dark wrists up to expose the darker welts, twisting her arms so I could see that the welts ran all around and rose most prominently over the bone where the ropes had cut the deepest.

"That's where he tied me up," she said. "And I could show you my cigarette burns too. You want to see them?"

Allerton slipped an arm around her, saying they had to return to the courtroom. But Powell was angry, passionate, almost fierce, as she shook her skinny, scarred arms in my face. "I'll tell you what you want to know," she said too loudly. "You won't hear it in that courtroom." Then Allerton coaxed Powell to dash some water on her hot face and asked me to leave. When Powell returned to the courtroom minutes later she was again subdued and rigid, her manner upright and thoroughly dignified with just a hint of contrition. In the lavatory I had seen a different Bernadette Powell, angry and deeply embittered; and perhaps because the person I encountered was so unexpected and unnerving, I put her out of my mind and instead watched closely the Bernadette Powell I observed in court. As I followed this case, that was the first mistake I made.

Chance brought me to that room in the Tompkins County Courthouse, chance and old friends who happened to live in Ithaca. They knew that for years I had been working on a book about women who commit homicide. They knew that I was writing a chapter about battered women who kill their assailants—their husbands and boyfriends—in self-defense. When they read in the local paper that a man named Herman Smith had been shot and killed by his former wife, Bernadette Powell, a battered woman, they telephoned me.

I missed the jury selection, but of the trial itself I heard every word and took notes. Watching so closely, I observed certain things that later, when I went on to other work, I did not forget. I remembered Bernadette Powell's dignity and her plain suffering. I remembered Al Smith, the key prosecution witness (though no relation to the dead Herman), squirming on the witness stand, twisting this way and that, a painful embodiment of his own devious story, as though his words had become his flesh and he was doomed to act them out. I remembered Diane Nelson, testifying for the prosecution, languid, apparently stoned, snapping her chewing gum to cover her nervousness, a disreputable woman, I thought, who would say anything, do anything, to get by.

I remembered Powell's court-appointed counsel, Dirk Galbraith, with lean, tailored suits and platinum hair. (It wasn't quite platinum, of course, but so it came to seem with the hyperbole of memory.) I remembered how he stood so stiffly away from Bernadette, how he would talk to her confidentially without bringing his face close to hers, without ever laying a reassuring hand on her arm, a curiously fastidious attorney who didn't like his client and who, through a certain diffidence, let the jury know that if it were up to him he'd have a better one, more respectable, certainly more innocent.

I remembered the prosecuting attorney, D.A. Joe Joch, rumpled and eager, hollow eyed and hungry looking, a terrier to Galbraith's well-groomed afghan, nasty in his innuendos, cozying up to the little clique seated around the foreman in the middle of the jury box, like the good ol' boys in the locker room. I remembered a half hour in Joch's office upstairs, above the courtroom, after a long day, when he leaned back behind his big desk and gradually waxed expansive about his record and his hopes to become a judge on the family-court bench. As the interview was winding down, I asked, "Would you care to comment on the allegations that you beat your wife?" I remembered how his feet hit the floor and his hands slammed down onto the desk in fists.

Bernadette Powell was convicted of murdering her ex-husband, and I went back to New York City, to the writers' study in the public library, where the worst quarrels concerned smoking habits and just how far the window should be opened; and there I finished writing *Women Who Kill.* I heard that Powell was sentenced to fifteen years to life. I went on the road for a month in 1980 and again in 1981 doing publicity for *Women Who Kill,* and during radio and television interviews I sometimes talked about the case of Bernadette Powell, as I talked about many other cases that left justice wanting. Whenever I did, kindhearted people who did not know Bernadette Powell, or me either, sent money from Seattle or Atlanta or Cleveland to the Bernadette Powell Defense Fund. To Bernadette Powell herself, who was by that time in prison, they sent notes, many of them printed out with difficulty, saying things like, "Sister, take heart. God sees you."

I remembered too a long afternoon I spent interviewing the ex-wife of D.A. Joch. We sat down together in her immaculate living room, and she told me all about her marriage, even showed me the contusions in the wallboard in the hallway and where the blood had spattered near the telephone. She told the story dramatically, perhaps melodramatically. She was, by training, an actress. And she told it in almost stupefying detail, recalling and describing each nuance of voice and movement with the subtlety and singlemindedness of a novelist. That clarity comes from the need to survive. Almost any battered woman, ready to dodge or run, can tell you precisely when his voice rose a tone, when his hand clenched, when his jaw tightened, and just exactly how his eyebrows lowered a moment before the first blow came down. Marie DeJong-Joch told me that kind of story.

Remembering, I wrote an article for a New York City publication, the *Soho Weekly News,* about the issues involved in the appeal of Bernadette Powell's conviction. Martin Stolar, the attorney hired by the Bernadette Powell Defense Fund to handle the appeal, argued, as I had argued on radio and TV, that Powell should get a new trial because the prosecutor had acted improperly. He should have excused himself from the case, Stolar said, because as an accused wife beater he appeared to have a personal interest in the key issue of battering. Whoever wrote the headlines at the *Soho Weekly News* titled my article CAN A WIFE BEATER PROSECUTE A BATTERED WIFE FOR KILLING A WIFE BEATER? By chance the piece appeared the week before Joe Joch stood for reelection as Tompkins County district attorney, but whether anyone in Ithaca read the *Soho Weekly News*, whether the article played any part in his surprising defeat, I never knew. But Joch lost the election—and Powell lost her appeal.

That was all there was to it, and that would have been the end of it if my friends in Ithaca had not gone away for the summer of 1982 and asked me to look after their house and animals. That's how I happened to be in Ithaca again when a hearing was held in county court on another of Marty Stolar's motions to set aside the conviction of Bernadette Powell and give her a new trial, this time because Stolar had discovered some startling new evidence that might have changed the verdict if only the jurors had heard it at the trial. That's how I happened to be in court when a young woman named Cynthia Shuford told a story that didn't match the prosecution's case against Bernadette Powell. That's how I happened to be invited after the hearing to a celebratory lunch at the Moosewood Restaurant. That's how I happened to invite Rebecca Allerton, who had become a leader of the Bernadette Powell Defense Fund, to come take a dip in my pond. "It's such a relief to *know*," she said that day. "I used to think I'd go through my whole life and never really know what happened between Herman and Bernadette. But now, at last, with Cynthia Shuford's testimony, to *know* what happened, to really *know* is such a relief!" And then Marty Stolar called to say that the judge's decision had gone against Powell, and Allerton went away quickly hiding angry tears.

I too was angry, and amazed. I knew that most Americans believe, as I used to, that a person falsely convicted can simply appeal that decision. Whenever I spoke publicly about the miscarriage of justice in one case or another—about mistaken identity, misleading circumstantial evidence, perjured testimony, inept counsel, the biases of the law itself, or simple human error—people in the audience were bound to say, "Well, that's a shame. That'll get appealed." The appeal seems to many to be a process both automatic and magical by which the criminal justice system redresses its own occasional mistakes—hence the label *justice*. But in fact the appeal of injustice is not automatic. It takes money, lots of it, for lawyers, and an unconscionable amount of time. It usually is concerned not with the substance of the case but with its form, not with the wisdom or justice of the verdict, but with the correctness of the trial procedure. And the decisions of the higher courts more often than not are dictated by the terrible constraints of the legal brotherhood. What the lower court has decreed, the higher court may not easily put aside, for they are all in it together, this criminal justice "system." The higher courts must reverse enough decisions to maintain public confidence in that system, but not enough to undermine it.

So after the hearing on Powell's second motion for a new trial, Judge William Barrett upheld the original guilty verdict reached in the trial court of Judge Bruce Dean. The appellate division of the New York State Supreme Court would uphold Judge Barrett, and the state Court of Appeals would find no reason to hear a case so well disposed of by the lower courts. The same decisions had been handed down before, the first time around. Whether Powell's attorney raised issues of trial procedure (the prosecutor's misconduct) or of substance (the new testimony of Cynthia Shuford), the result was the same. How was a person unfairly caught up in the criminal justice system ever to be freed?

Months later, I came across the case of Lenell Geter, a young black engineer in Texas who had the bad habit of going to a public park during his lunch hour to eat and read a book. Thus, his car, parked daily where it "didn't belong," was reported to the police, and his license number was plugged into the computer when suspects were sought in the armed robbery of a fried-chicken shack. Lenell Geter was arrested, identified in a lineup, tried, and, despite the testimony of colleagues who were with him at work fifty miles away at the time of the crime, convicted and sentenced to life imprisonment for "his" first offense. Even after other co-workers came forward to protest, even after the CBS news program "Sixty Minutes" exposed the mistake, the local prosecutor told the press he was sure he "had the right man." The conviction was absurd, of course, but under normal circumstances it probably would have washed. Unfortunately for the Dallas County prosecutor, Lenell Geter was not just another poor look-alike black. He was an engineer, and the co-workers who knew he'd been in the office were white and respectable and hence, unlike poor blacks, not to be ignored. Besides, after "Sixty Minutes," the governor got involved. It was making Texas look bad, to be found out that way. So they had to offer Lenell Geter a new trial and release him from prison after he'd served only a little more than a year of his life sentence.*

Americans clamor for law and order. We may overlook those criminals who rob, defraud, and kill us by thousands—the corporate executives and their political allies who commit Three Mile Island, thalidomide, DES, Rely tampons, Agent Orange, and the Ford Pinto—but we cry out for protection from random criminals in the streets. Overwhelmed by the crimes of increasingly violent men, increasingly poor and desperate women, Americans understandably want to be "safe." The government says the problem is "the

---

*Cases like Geter's are not rare. Nathaniel Carter, convicted in Queens in 1982 of murdering his ex-wife's foster mother and sentenced to twenty-five years to life, served two years before his ex-wife confessed to the crime. In his case, witnesses who could have provided an alibi were not called to testify.

criminal element," not poverty and hopelessness, and it be-
gins again to fry men and women to demonstrate that criminals, regardless of how they may have been made, can be
unmade by a simple electrical procedure.

How can we be so certain and so righteous? How could
we condemn for life a woman as battered and beset by
misfortune as Bernadette Powell? How could we lock up
for life a man convicted of one armed robbery? And how
could we ignore it when witnesses came forward to say,
"You've got the wrong person"? Lenell Geter was offered
a new trial. Didn't the state of Texas owe him more than
that—restitution, or at the very least an apology? But Bernadette Powell could not even get a new trial. New evidence in her case was simply discounted as not important
enough, not of the "quality" given at the trial, somehow
suspect.

As I thought about it, I grew angrier, until one day, when
Rebecca Allerton came again to swim in the pond, I told
her I might write a book about the Powell case, just to
indicate how subject to error the process of American "justice" is. It made me particularly angry, I explained, that
although Cynthia Shuford came forward with a new story
suggesting Powell's innocence, showing that things had happened quite differently from the prosecutor's version of events,
the court could disregard her testimony.

Allerton was quiet for a long time as we swam and sat
in the sun. But quietness was her habit. I read a book, certain
she must be floating in her own daydreams. But later, as we
walked to her car, she suddenly said with great seriousness
what she must have been pondering all along. "Before you
take up this issue, I think you probably should know that
some people say Cynthia Shuford is not such a disinterested
witness."

"How so?"

"Well, there's talk that she actually is the girl friend of
Bernadette's brother Oscar Lee."

"You're kidding," I protested. "I saw them at that lunch

at Moosewood after the hearing, and they didn't seem to know each other at all."

"That's what I thought, too. But the investigator Marty Stolar hired picked up this other story, from more than one source. I just thought you should know."

"Rebecca, this is serious stuff. How long have you known this?"

"I don't *know* it. It's just what I hear. But I thought I'd better tell you."

"How long?" I insisted, but she was already going down the drive.

Was it true? And what did it mean? Did it mean that this was not, after all, a simple case of injustice? Or was it a simple case of injustice complicated by a clumsy attempt to set it straight? Perhaps I'd have to write another article called CAN A WOMAN CONVICTED BY FALSE EVIDENCE MAKE UP FALSE EVIDENCE TO REVERSE HER CONVICTION? But I was getting ahead of myself. Suppose Shuford was Oscar Lee's girl friend. Did that mean her testimony had to be false? If it was false, who invented it? If someone invented it, who else knew about it? And if Shuford's testimony contradicting the prosecution witnesses was trumped up, was it possible that what those witnesses said at the trial was true after all?

Behind the "facts" lay problems too complicated for the simple adversarial system of criminal justice. In court you are guilty or not guilty, right or wrong. You win or you lose, or your lawyer wins or loses. There is nothing in between. So lawyers don't care much for the truth of what happened. They want only a version of the "truth," a story that will fly in a court of law. If the true story is a loser, then they must improve upon it or pare it down or stand it on end, or persuade the client to plea bargain and avoid the courtroom altogether. In this way legal advocacy obscures reality. How much "truth" lay in the stories defense attorney Galbraith and prosecutor Joch told the jury in 1979? What *was* the truth and where had it gotten lost? And could it be recovered?

Two days later Allerton telephoned. "Have you given it up?"

"Not a chance. You shatter my simple views of right and wrong and expect me to sit here quietly with my hands folded? I have to know what's going on."

"You could be real sorry."

"I'm already sorry. But I'm going to go into it myself."

I did go into it. And the more I waded the waters, the murkier they became.

In my investigations I tried to be scrupulous. I talked to the family and close friends of Bernadette Powell. I talked to the foster family and close friends and lovers of Herman Smith, the man Powell married, the man she killed. I talked to the defense attorney and to the prosecutor. I talked to the defense witnesses and to the chief witnesses for the prosecution. I talked to the state police experts and to the women of the Bernadette Powell Defense Fund. I talked to the jurors and the judges and the private investigators. I talked to a man who fell in love with Bernadette Powell inside the county jail and to a woman who fell in love with her inside the state prison.

I talked, for as many hours as the prison would allow, to Powell herself; and from the beginning, she encouraged me. In long, wearying interviews and correspondence she dredged her memory in search of what we both called then, in our innocence, "the truth." Much of the personal history she shared with me was palpably painful to her. Of the "bad" things she had done in her life—most of them commonplace sins—she was deeply ashamed. Yet she told me about them, though she had nothing to gain by doing so but that "truth" we kept looking for. (I report those "bad" things with real trepidation, knowing they may well count against Bernadette Powell now in the eyes of those functionaries of the state who still control her future—judges, members of the parole board, and the governor of New York. In particular, the physical fights in which Powell was involved, though routine for any young man living in her circumstances, may seem evidence to middle class observers of a violent and dangerous nature simply because they are not "ladylike.")

Partisans on both sides of the Powell case talked among themselves. They did not cross the lines drawn between them. I seemed to be the only person who talked with the head of the Bernadette Powell Defense Fund and then walked across the street to the black Elks Club to talk to the chief prosecution witnesses. For months I talked to anyone who would talk to me, so that in the end I knew more than anyone else about the case.

But I knew next to nothing. I never found out what happened. I still don't know the "truth," and I feel sure that I never will.

Instead I pieced together the stories of some people whose lives were warped by rigid conventions of race and sex and class, people who tried so hard to be what they "should" that they lost track of who they were, people who tried so hard to impose their own stories, their own expectations, upon others that they could not see what lay before their eyes. I started out self-righteously to tell a story of simple injustice, but when I found injustice it was not simple. It came in layers, settling like sediment. It had no sides or right angles. Once laid down, it tended to keep piling up. Often it was precipitated by people with the best intentions. And it could grow adamant as rock.

I came away with a fear of righteousness and anger, wherever I found it—in the judge and jurors, in the D.A., in Bernadette Powell, in myself. In the end it seemed to me that all our systems and our institutions for "dealing with" people are makeshift contraptions, cut to fit our prejudices and expectations, prefabricated to shelter and contain us, to save us from genuine human concern, to spare us alike the suffering we might see and the love we might achieve. The story of Bernadette Powell is a story of failures of human concern, failures of love. People failed her—her father and mother, her husband, her friends, her lawyer, her judge. Institutions failed her—the schools, the social services, the courts, the prisons. Even the women of the Bernadette Powell Defense Fund, though they cared for her very well, got her wrong. Maybe, as those who wrote to her in prison said, God saw Bernadette Powell. Nobody else did.

I caught only glimpses of her, and of Herman, two troubled people ensnared, like kidnapped sleepers, in other people's hand-me-down dreams, prisoners of patterns of race and class and sex and store-bought ambitions. "You shouldn't write about them," Everett Jackson, Herman's foster father, commanded me. "You should write about somebody successful, somebody who's a model for youngsters. Herman and Bernadette were nobodys. They never would have amounted to anything, either one of them. They're bad examples, very bad examples. They're just everyday Americans."

An eminent legal scholar also advised me not to write about this case. "It doesn't *make* law," she said. "There's nothing new here, and no general applicability. It's not even a typical battered woman's self-defense case; the facts are too iffy, too much open to question. It's just another ordinary murder case."

This book is about that ordinary murder case and some of the people it touched, especially two "everyday Americans"—one shot to death and the other imprisoned for at least fifteen years, possibly for the rest of her life.

CHAPTER 1

# BERNADETTE

From the beginning Bernadette Alyce Powell was her father's little girl. She was born in Binghamton, New York, in the spring of 1952, less than a year after her mother, Margie Fields, dropped out of Central High at age seventeen to marry a handsome nineteen-year-old truck driver, Oscar Lee Powell. He was a stocky, good-looking man with a smooth laugh; and he could drive enormous machines—earthmovers and giant caterpillars—as though they were toys. Those early days were happy, but they didn't last. Soon there were quarrels and blows and tears and screaming, and then her father wasn't at home anymore. He came to see Bernadette sometimes and always he whispered in her ear, so no one else could hear, that someday he would come and take her away. She yearned for that day, and she waited, but his visits dwindled until at last she hardly ever saw him anymore. She walked blocks and blocks to the house where he lived, and she pounded on the door until the light-skinned woman came and stood behind the screen and said that Bernadette's daddy wasn't home and that she mustn't come here looking for him anymore. Bernadette stood on the sloping porch listening to the message she had heard before, peering through the rusty impenetrable screen as though she might just make out the form of her daddy where she knew he lay on the couch in the darkened room behind.

Then her mother left her, too. Margie was always in and out of the hospital suffering illnesses the doctors could never quite identify, in and out of jobs—housecleaner, shoe factory worker, deliveryperson—trying to get some money for the kids. There were four of them now. She left them with her mama and papa at their farm out in Johnson City, and there, sometimes for months, sometimes for a year or two, Bernadette and her little brother Oscar Lee, Jr., and the others waited to be reclaimed.

Barbara and Leslie Fields, Bernadette's grandparents, headed one of the oldest black families in the valley. Barbara, the matriarch of the clan, was born in 1915 in Troy, Alabama, the daughter of a woodcutter and his third wife, a washerwoman. At fourteen Barbara married Leslie Fields, an eighteen-year-old handyman who attended the "colored" high school. When he graduated as valedictorian he and Barbara already had three children, and he already anticipated trouble from the white woman who employed him. Quickly, without announcing his departure, Leslie left town to follow Barbara's oldest stepbrother, a minister, north to Binghamton. There he was still a handyman, but on safer ground. Six months later, in the winter of 1934, he sent for his wife, and just before her nineteenth birthday she boarded the express train in Bessemer, Alabama, with three small children. The baby in her arms, her third child, Marjorie, only six months old and severely ill with pneumonia, would be sickly all her life, but in her time, she became the mother of Bernadette Powell.

Barbara and Leslie Fields became part of the historic black migration from south to north. Binghamton, their new home, was at the heart of what local boosters liked to call the Valley of Opportunity, a fortunate hub of transportation and manufacture two hundred miles by rail or river from the sea, sixty miles as the crow flies from Appalachian coal. The industrial revolution made it a boomtown. By the 1920s the Valley of Opportunity boasted 258 factories turning out the goods of expansive capitalism—shoes and silk, cigars, time clocks, and tabulating instruments. The chamber of commerce described life in Binghamton like this: ". . . with all our industries we have a spotless community. . . . Here we mow and water our close-clipped lawns and tend our little gardens. . . . Here we alternately toil and rest, strive and enjoy the fruits of striving, love and hate, quarrel and make up. For we are as other folks, here in the Valley of Opportunity, and have our share of the frailties common to mankind."

One of those frailties was a certain clannishness, an unwillingness to share the blessings of opportunity with all comers. The chamber of commerce took pride that the "foreign element" in their well-scrubbed city was "small . . . only eleven percent of the population." Most of that foreign element was Italian. Of the seventy churches in Binghamton in the twenties—mostly Methodist, Presbyterian, and Baptist—ten were Catholic, two were "African," and one "Jewish." To discourage the foreign element the Ku Klux Klan maintained a large chapter, particularly active in 1928 when a Catholic, Al Smith, was nominated for governor of New York. In 1934 when young Barbara Fields stepped off the train carrying her sick baby, there were well over 100,000 people in the Valley of Opportunity, but only a few hundred of them were black.

They were not allowed to work in factories or skilled trades, so Leslie Fields found handyman's work as a janitor at the gas company. The Fieldses joined the black Baptist church, where Leslie sang in the gospel quartet, the Harps of David, and worked his way up to the office of deacon. They moved from one small apartment to the next, always downtown in the flats along the river, the part of town reserved for the Italians and the "colored." And the children came, one after another, almost every year. At last there were eight girls, like stair steps, and three boys scattered among them almost forgotten while the children became known collectively around town as "the Fields sisters," the name spoken with respect and some fear. At last the doctor told Barbara she should have no more children. After sixteen pregnancies—eleven children and five miscarriages—she had a tubal ligation. She was thirty-two years old.

The Fieldses worked fourteen years to buy, in 1948, a house on Susquehanna Street, a two-story tenement with railroad flats up and down, the little parade of rooms marching front to back. Barbara used them all, put big double beds even in the hallways so she could sleep everybody, even when the girls were grown and straggled back to their mama's after a bad beating. From time to time they came with their children to be taken in while they sorted things out, got back on their feet. Bernadette came to Susquehanna Street as a young girl with her mother Margie and her brother Oscar Lee after her father kicked Margie in the stomach. Susquehanna Street was where you went if your mama's name was Fields and you had some trouble.

In the sixties the Susquehanna Street neighborhood fell to urban renewal. A white clergyman, Reverend Darling, suggested in 1959 that the mayor appoint a committee of citizens (white) who could "talk their language" (black) to discover an area of the city (preferably remote) where blacks could live "by themselves." "I have some very good friends locally in the city who are Negroes," he said, "and they don't want to go into places where whites do not want them. They want to be together." The federal Model Cities Program—urban renewal—seemed to be the answer. So the city fathers leveled tenements to make way for public buildings and new apartments that would house fewer people, people with higher incomes. They demolished neighborhood grocery stores and bars and clubs. They shoved out longtime residents and offered them housing in projects scattered around the city's periphery, far from transportation and jobs. They dispersed the blacks of Susquehanna Street—some 90 percent of Binghamton's black population—and to prevent their gathering together again they built intersecting expressways to dismember the old neighborhood. Susquehanna was not so much a street anymore but an exit ramp. When the black people saw what had been done to them, they began to speak of the program as "urban removal." Then it went awry, dwindled, and stopped. The Fields house and a few other buildings on Susquehanna Street were left standing in the midst of vacant lots just off the intersection of the expressways, a few blocks from the massive state office building, the showpiece of the master plan, an eighteen-story civic joke, deserted after an electrical fire because certain toxic chemicals make it unfit for human life.

Barbara and Leslie Fields left Susquehanna Street in 1964 and bought a farm several miles outside of town near the village of Johnson City. They were the only black people in the township. They had thirty-five acres and a brokendown farmhouse at the end of a deserted road. For the next twenty years it was the Fields family headquarters, full of emergencies and sorrow and smiling color photographs ranked on the bookcase and the television set, photographs of the grandchildren. (Leslie Fields never could remember whether there were sixty-five or sixty-eight of them, all told.) It was a house full of couches and beds to be used by children and grandchildren with no place else to go. It harbored the children of daughter Margie—Bernadette, Oscar Lee, Tonya—while Margie worked in Binghamton at the best job she ever had: secretary in the office of the Model Cities Program.

In 1970 Leslie Fields, who had been a maintenance man at the Security Mutual Insurance Company for "thirty-some" years, heard God call him—like his father before him—to be a minister. For four years, while he continued to work in maintenance, he took evening classes at the Practical Bible School in Johnson City. In 1974, at age sixty-two, he was ordained and within a year he founded his own church in Binghamton. He named it Our Free Will Baptist Church, which signifies that anyone who has the will is free to join. "Dedicated to all races and creeds from every walk of life," it has about 150 members, all black, and almost all women.

The Reverend Fields so perfectly exemplifies the all-American virtues of hard work, thrift, humility, and Christian faith, that in 1969, at a surprise birthday party in his honor, the mayor of Binghamton named him an Outstanding Citizen and gave him the keys to the city. That, of course, was long before his granddaughter Bernadette was arrested for murder. But afterward, in 1980, the congregation gave a banquet at the Ramada Inn to honor him and to observe the fifth anniversary of Our Free Will Baptist Church and the fiftieth wedding anniversary of the Reverend Fields and his wife. Fellow ministers came from Corning and Elmira and Rochester, and an officer of the Urban League came all the way from New York City to pay tribute to him. He is a handsome, powerful, barrel-chested man looking decades younger than his age, deep-voiced and riveted by an anger so profound, so well grounded, and so perfectly unconscious that he appears to be blessedly driven by the spirit of the Lord.

In his stern household Bernadette and her brothers and sister waited until Margie picked up a job in a bar on Susquehanna Street and found an apartment for them. She took up with one of the bar owners, a guy named Richard, who was nice to Bernadette. Even though he wasn't really her father, he sometimes pretended to be, until Margie bore him two kids who were, as they said, "really his," and then he didn't pay much attention to Bernadette and Oscar Lee and the others anymore. This time Bernadette saw the blows. She saw Richard push her mother down the stairs, and she remembered her falling, falling. When Margie came home from the hospital Richard was gone and she did not seem to be at all the same person, having suffered a cerebral hemorrhage. After that Margie sat in a chair and swallowed a lot of pills and took the world's measure.

She didn't like it much. And she didn't understand why it had gone against her. Once she had been one of the powerful Fields sisters. Nobody messed with the Fields sisters. But somebody had. A couple of men had. And now she was stuck at home with her kids and her endless supply of pills. Not that her sisters hadn't had their troubles. Was there one of them who hadn't gotten tied up with some man who liked to beat on women? Still, the others seemed to have come out of it better. They'd remarried, some of them to wimpy white men who weren't quite so quick with the punches; and they had good jobs, nice homes, fancy furniture, new cars. They dressed well and they dressed their kids well. They hung around together and drank in the clubs and laughed a lot and worked for CORE and the NAACP. They were the Fields sisters and they did as they pleased and nobody messed with them—at least not for long.

Somehow Margie didn't seem to be one of them anymore, but she had high hopes for her daughter Bernadette. Little Bernie, as Margie called her—she had nicknames for all her children—was so cute and so "petee." She had such a sense of style, such a way with clothes, and so much vitality. People just naturally noticed her, and they liked her. Little Bernie tried out for the color guard at high school and made the squad, the first black girl ever to do so, and Margie just knew she had a special child, a child who would put all the Fields sisters to shame.

In 1964, when Bernadette was twelve years old and staying with her grandparents in Johnson City, she enrolled for the sixth grade in the Maine Township Memorial School. She was a smiling child with neatly pressed hair, and according to her supervising teacher "very well adjusted." She "made friends easily," the teacher reported, and was "treated as an equal by her peers." She made an "excellent effort" and performed with "average ability in most subjects" although she was "below average in math." At the end of the school year her teachers evaluated her as an "eager" student, "completely dependable," "willing," and "a steady worker." She was "well balanced," they said, "courteous," a "good mixer" who showed "deep concern" for others. In all her courses except French, to which she remained "indifferent," she received A's and B's. Despite this achievement, Bernadette, the only black pupil in her class, was switched onto the "Local" track, channeled into a curriculum designed for the "lowest 20 percent" of students, those who would not receive "average" preparation for the Regents Exam and college entrance and who would never, by the most ambitious leap, attain "honors."

Within the year she left Maine Memorial to live with her mother in Binghamton. A year later she was back at Maine, and a month later she moved back to Binghamton, bound to record in her school transfers the emotional disjunctions of her mother's life. What did it matter? Applying the most up-to-date educational tracking techniques, the schools had already recognized her eager, childish aspirations and systematically blocked them.

When she reached Binghamton's North High, one of the nineteen black students in a class of twelve hundred, she, like all the other black girls, was tracked into the "commercial" course. Margie hoped that her ambitious, promising daughter would go to college, and Bernadette herself longed for college and a career in journalism. But it was hard for Margie, after her troubles, to get out to visit Bernadette's teachers. It was hard for Margie to understand what went into college preparation. Wasn't preparing for college what you did when you went to high school? In Bernadette's case—in the case of all the black students at North High—it was not.

Her high school friends remember Bernadette as a ball of fire, energetic, eager, high-spirited, and a hard worker. Still it's hard to imagine how she got into the color guard, being "colored" in the wrong sense; but after she wore slacks to school one day, the principal had an excuse to kick her off the squad before she actually appeared in public. (Rebellious, she showed up for her graduation ceremonies wearing slacks under her gown.) Thinking the experience of speaking in public would be good training for a journalist—especially one considering broadcast journalism—she joined the drama club, but the school plays had no parts for black students, and she always wound up painting the scenery. Somehow all her energy always carried her headlong into that place where there was no room for her. Brought up short again and again, baffled, casting about for something to engage fully her ebullient spirit, she did not know that the barrier she met was racism. A few black students at North High called for a student walkout to support their demands: for a black literature course, parts for black students in plays and offices on the student council, college-prep tracking for eligible blacks. Teachers said the protest was the work of "outside agitators" and lamented that so few students up in arms could put the whole school through *that*. When they asked loyal "colored" students to remain in the classroom, Bernadette remained.

Bewildered and vaguely frustrated, she got all dressed up one day and went with some girl friends to a bar on Susquehanna Street. She was wearing some tight tomboy pants and cute white boots with tassels, and she knew she looked good, but still she was surprised when she glanced over her shoulder to see the way that new guy at the end of the bar stared at her. His shirt was open, and when he came close she could see that on his dark chest he had a tattoo.

Bernadette admired her grandmother Fields more than anyone in the world, but for as long as she could remember she'd been afraid of turning out like the other women in the family, the women of her mother's generation. Self-sufficient as they seemed to be, she knew they all had devoted their lives to men who took their money and their self-respect, gave them children and little else, abused them, beat them, left them, usually with the bills unpaid. They talked tough, but like her mother they raged and cried in the night. And they competed among themselves. Who had the nicest house, the best furniture, the flashiest clothes, the biggest car? Surely there was another way to live. As a child she'd dreamed of escaping as a ballerina from Binghamton and the family's infighting, but no matter how often she pleaded, her mother never bought her the shoes. Perhaps journalism would take her away.

She hadn't planned on Hermie Smith and the way, when he looked at her, he could make her feel. She was a tomboy, yearning—without knowing how to plan—for a career. But maybe it was true after all, what she had been told, that a woman was just supposed to love a man and try to do for him and make him happy. When Hermie made love to her she was almost sure of it, and when she knew she was pregnant, she would have married him as he asked, if Margie hadn't taken her instead to Broome County Social Services. It would be such a disgrace, Margie said, if anyone found out. What would Margie's parents think, and her sisters? Margie would never live it down, nor Bernadette either. She was too young, not even finished with high school yet. And besides, Bernadette was going to college.

Bernadette dropped out of high school in October 1969, telling the school authorities that she was "moving to Buffalo," and went with a social worker to a home for unwed mothers in Utica. Herman found out where she was, and a couple of times he came to visit, thoughtfully bringing flowers as though she were suffering some disease or recuperating from an operation. They couldn't seem to talk about why they were not getting married and keeping the child; they couldn't quite figure it out. Still everything might have been all right if the nurses had not told Bernadette that her child was a boy and brought him in for her to hold. She gave him a name, and then the nurses took him away and she never saw him again.

Somehow after that nothing went quite right. She couldn't seem to focus. It was as though part of her went home from the hospital with her child, another part with her mother. Sometimes it almost seemed as if she would never come together again. Part of her wanted to spend her life with

Hermie. Part of her wanted to make an entirely new life, a career, for herself.

For a time she tried to do both. She went back to North High—and back to Herman Smith. When she had her picture taken with the drama group for the school yearbook, she was cutting up in the front row, striking a boyish pose, wearing an oversized T-shirt that belonged to her friend Hermie. She was pregnant again. By January 1971, when she graduated from North High, she had ended that pregnancy and another one by visiting a doctor, but she was still seeing Herman.

Through a special economic-opportunity program she won a scholarship to a business school—the only kind of "college" she was eligible for—in Rochester, New York. When she signed up for courses in basic typing and business math, she hoped to become a business executive; but the school was hard, too hard after North High where the black students were never expected to do much. Soon she was failing all her courses. And she was lonely, being away from home, among strangers. The dorm reminded her of the Utica home, and she didn't want to remember.

Herman didn't want to let her go. He came up every weekend, and she smuggled him into her room. He made love to her and talked about the other babies they would have and the house he would buy for her. One weekend she slipped out of the dorm with him. Some time before, on some ruse, they had taken the trouble to get her mother's signature. They used it then to obtain the license just over the state line in Pennsylvania, and they quickly married.

The two parts of Bernadette, like partners in a bad marriage, could not live together. She had given up a child to keep her dream of college. Now to keep Herman, she gave up college. And to make sense of her life, she began to forget part of it, the "bad" part. She forgot her firstborn child. She forgot her abortions. When she dropped out of business school in her first semester, she forgot that too. At her trial she testified under oath that she had borne only one child and that she was a graduate of the Rochester Business Institute. She wanted people to know only that she was educated, intelligent, proper, nice, several cuts above the people she came from and the life she wanted to leave behind. Herman Smith often embroidered upon the events of his life to make himself more manly and more colorful. Bernadette simply ignored in her life the events that seemed to her ignoble. Herman made up good stories. Bernadette put bad stories out of her mind. Herman invented. Bernadette forgot. In this stratagem her immediate family supported her, for they too valued the appearance of things.

Bernadette tried to make revenge of living well. She tried to create a life the Fields sisters and their daughters must envy—the suburban home, the fine furniture, the snappy sports car. Herman opened an auto reconditioning shop, and Bernadette worked hard at home, planning, buying, arranging, cleaning, keeping everything just so. She had it all. And a new baby too, a beautiful boy. But then the money ran short, and Herman started hitting her. At first she didn't tell anyone. She just went on cleaning her house. What mattered, after all, was not so much the marriage itself as what you had to show for it. He tied her up and hit her and kicked her down the stairs and held her under the scalding shower and locked her in the trunk of the car. Always, afterward, he was tearful and sorry. But always he did it again. And when he started attacking her in public—at her mother's, at the Ramada Inn and the Cadillac Lounge—she knew she had a "secret" she couldn't keep.

She thought the family—the Fields sisters—must be laughing at her. Just before Christmas in 1973, when she was twenty-one, Bernadette barged into her Aunt Dorthea's home in the middle of the day, swinging a broken pair of scissors. The weapon cut Dorthea's lip and struck her shoulder, but she managed to subdue her niece and had her arrested for assault in the third degree, a misdemeanor.

Bernadette claimed that "others" were planning to kill Dorthea anyway, so Bernadette might as well do it herself. To some members of the Fields family Bernadette seemed to be taking up her mother's quarrel with Dorthea where Margie, because of her illness, had been forced to leave off. Nobody quite remembered what that quarrel was about, although everyone thought it concerned, at least in part, the question of who was "queen" of the Fields sisters. Bernadette herself said that Dorthea had invited her over, then locked the door and attacked *her*. To Dorthea, Bernadette appeared to be "very mixed up" and in need of help, but under pressure from other members of the family she dropped her complaint, and the charge against Bernadette was dismissed. Perhaps at that point the family might have saved Bernadette. They chose instead to save face.

A few months later Bernadette went to Binghamton to find a lawyer, and in April 1974 the Broome County Court issued the first of many orders meant to protect Bernadette Smith from her violent husband. Two weeks later the court issued another order directing Herman not to "molest the petitioner in any way physically" for a year, and before the year was out it ordered him to "remain away from her premises" altogether for three months. In October 1975, Herman beat Bernadette badly, sending her to the hospital emergency room at three o'clock in the morning for skull and back X rays and treatment of multiple contusions. The next day he rampaged through the house and destroyed most of the furniture with a knife and a hammer, then fought with a policeman who tried to arrest him and cracked the officer's ribs. The court ordered him to leave home and "remain away" indefinitely. But he kept coming back until, at last, on July 6, 1977, the court ordered the marriage "dissolved." Bernadette Smith became Bernadette Powell once again.

She tried to carry on as though nothing really had happened. But she had to sell the "Spanish colonial" house in suburban Vestal—how was she to pay for it?—and move to a small apartment in Binghamton. From there she walked to her new job as an aide in a nursing home, but all the while she feared that Herman might be right behind her. Then one night she saw him laughing and drinking with two young women in a bar, and she knew she didn't want to see such a thing again. The next day she quit her job and took her son in the new car she bought with money from the sale of the Vestal house and went to Ithaca to look for a new place to live. She had gone to high school games once or twice in Ithaca, and she thought it seemed like a nice town, cleaner and smaller than Binghamton, a town where she would not get lost. She put the rest of the money from the house sale—a few thousand dollars—in an envelope to take along, just in case she needed it. But she was upset, and when she stopped to take the child to the ladies' room in the Binghamton bus station, she left the envelope there. That was a stupid thing to do, she knew, and pointless to report to the police, but it was the way things had been going for a while. It was about as haphazard as her move to Ithaca.

When she reached Ithaca, Bernadette drove aimlessly around until she spotted a black man and a black woman chatting in front of a house across the street from the black Elks Club. She pulled up and asked if they knew of any inexpensive apartments for rent in the town. They did. The woman lived in a project where Bernadette might easily find an apartment. Diane Nelson and Ralph Brown got in Bernadette's car and directed her to the West Village Apartments, a federally subsidized low-income housing project.

Once Bernadette was settled, everyone acknowledged that her apartment was the showplace of West Village. Some of her furniture was old, she said (though she didn't often admit it), but she credited its fine condition to her own unsurpassed powers as a cleaner. Cleaning, she said at her trial, was her "drug." It also brought her status. But after a while she grew more and more tired. It wasn't that she was bored with cleaning—it was in fact the mindlessness of it that appealed to her—but she felt weary. It seemed easier then, once she had cleaned some part of the house until it was perfect, to set it aside so it wouldn't get dirty again. First she marked the living room off limits and took guests into the extra bedroom, fixed up as a dining room. When someone spilled soda on the rug, she put that room off limits, too. Then she closed off the living area and entertained guests around the bar in the kitchen. She stopped serving fluids, which might so easily be spilled.

In the time she saved by these measures, she slept. She put her son outside on the terrace or in the yard, so he wouldn't disturb anything in the house, and she slept. Late in the evening, about nine o'clock or so, she would get up and let the boy in and feed him in the kitchen and put him to bed. Her sister Tonya asked her to take care of her daughter for a while, so for a few months the boy had someone to play with while Bernadette slept.

She moved in to the West Village in September 1977, into a three-bedroom apartment which would have rented for $354 on the open market. The federal government offered a monthly subsidy of $151, and the county social services paid the rest. Bernadette listed her projected annual income at $4160 to be provided by "Welfare." (In fact they granted her $377 per month.) Her family, she wrote, consisted of herself, her five-year-old son, and her two-year-old "daughter," and that entitled her to receive each month $138 worth of food stamps.

She lived this way for six months, always wanting to rise above it and trying, through the simplest of the ways she knew, to find a meal ticket. At a bar she met a Cornell graduate student named Ron, who seemed to be an intellectual and an articulate theorist in black politics. Many other grad students thought Ron was all talk, a glib con man, but to Bernadette he was "brilliant"; and she always looked up to brilliant people, people who seemed to have all the answers to questions she couldn't even formulate.

That was the life she wanted for her son. Ron took her to lectures she couldn't understand and introduced her to sauterne. He was, she says, her first lover after Herman, and one of the most important men in her life. But when he went away, after a time, to attend another school, she didn't know where he was going or when or even where he was from. Bernadette's neighbors and friends in West Village don't remember Ron at all. They speak instead of other men, shadier and sometimes very young, but these Bernadette has put out of her mind.

Early in March 1978, six months after she moved into West Village, Bernadette advised the social services department that she no longer needed public assistance. "George Nikens from Harding Bros. of Elmira is now supporting me," she wrote, "and soon we'll be married." Two weeks later she wrote again: "My friend whom is George Nickens was not able to take me and mine due to lack of funds. Please void the closing of my case. Please continue my grant." In the meantime Bernadette went to work as an "Encapsulation Operator" in the "Aerospace Manufacturing Organization" of IBM thirty miles away in Owego. Her starting salary was $173.60 per week or approximately $9,027 per year. She did not tell social services about that. Nor did she tell them that her niece had gone back to Binghamton.

In fact, ten days later, Bernadette reapplied for welfare money saying that "just this month I dropped myself from assistance because I thought I was going to get help from a boyfriend he lied." She knew how things were supposed to go. She was supposed to "do" for some man, and he was supposed to give her money. But Herman hadn't always come up with the money, and it was harder than she had thought it would be to find another man to do for who would in turn provide for her and the child. She needed help, she wrote to social services, because she was one month behind on her rent, but she wouldn't need help for long. In

June, she said, "I'm going to leave Ithaca and better my life."

Nevertheless, in June she applied again. Her household, she told the social worker, had "no income of any kind." Her only resources, she said, were $2.75 in cash. But the department of social services, knowing that Bernadette was earning unreported income, was preparing a case to recover $1075.68 in payments she had accepted since she started working at IBM in March. On May 31, 1978, the department sent notice to Powell at IBM of its intent to discontinue her benefits. After June 9, the letter informed her, the Tompkins County Social Services would no longer support her or her children. Frightened, Bernadette notified the department only a week after reapplying for aid that she had just found a job.

Ithaca was shutting down. Social Services cut her off. If she didn't come up with the rent, West Village would kick her out of the apartment at the end of the month. What did she care? She had never wanted to live that way. Like Diane Nelson and her friend Lisa Johnson and the rest of them. She was used to better things. The better life.

She had been, all along, preparing for it. She went down to Owego in February and got the very first job she interviewed for at IBM. She found a realtor and a perfect house and filled out all the forms for the bank and the Farmers Home Administration and did everything just exactly right, just as the realtor told her to do. And she went to the Credit Union at IBM and filled out all the applications there and got the money for the closing on the house and also the money for a new pickup truck. And she found the truck and did all the paperwork on that. And all that time she'd been driving back and forth to work at night, almost an hour each way, and taking care of her son and walking him to school and baseball practice and karate class. When you thought about it, that was really quite a lot for any one person to do. When you thought about it, it almost seemed as if she didn't need Herman or Ron or George or even the welfare. It almost seemed as though she could do for herself.

It was what she said she wanted—just to work hard and make a nice home for her son, give him a better life. That's what she said to Stephanie, the realtor, who thought her an especially devoted mother. She showed Stephanie the boy's report card. That's what she told Detective Fanara of the Endicott Police when she had to report that Herman had teenagers in to smoke marijuana; and the detective too was impressed with her concern for other youngsters as well as her own child. That's what she told Tom Wallace, the nice middle-aged man she met in the IBM cafeteria, who was so impressed with her courage that he offered to rent her a spare bedroom in his apartment until she could move into her own house. At least it would save her the commuting.

On Saturday night, May 27, 1978, she threw a goodbye party for herself at her own apartment. She wanted everyone in West Village to know she was moving out, moving up. People packed into the apartment and drank and danced and carried on until almost four in the morning when Bud Ackerman, the West Village security man, came in and pulled the plug on the stereo. The next day around noon Jim McNeil, who lived just a few doors away, came banging on the door, wanting back a record he'd brought to the party. Bernadette said she didn't have his record, and he said she was trying to steal it, and then things rapidly got out of hand. Jim McNeil picked up a bottle—there were a lot of empties outside Powell's apartment that morning—and threw it at her as she stood in the doorway, yelling at him. It bounced off the door and struck her son, standing behind her, in the head, knocking him down. Powell snatched up a knife from the kitchen counter and charged at McNeil, but security man Ackerman, drawn by the sound of the quarrel, caught and disarmed her. Powell went to the phone and called Ralph Brown for help while McNeil ran off and returned with a lead pipe; but the police were right behind him to break up the fight. That afternoon the little boy fainted, and an ambulance took him to the hospital. Powell drove to Endicott to tell Herman. That evening two men and a woman some identified as Bernadette Powell jumped Jimmy McNeil and his girl friend in the street and beat him up. On Monday, May 29, both Powell's little boy and Jimmy McNeil were released from Tompkins County Hospital, and McNeil appeared in City Court along with Bernadette Powell, charged with menacing, a misdemeanor, to be lectured and dismissed.

The next day, too weary to clean up her apartment again, Powell put her furniture into storage, locked the door, and took the boy over to her friend Diane Nelson's. She put on rubber gloves and washed the walls in Diane's bedroom with Comet and made herself at home. That would have to do until she could get out of Ithaca to start her better life.

Still it was hard to start over. So she agreed to have Lisa Johnson stay with her in Owego for a little while, and one day they drove down there with the children and moved some things into Tom Wallace's apartment. That was just temporary, you understand. Until her house was ready. But things didn't work out with Lisa, either—everybody knew *she* was crazy—and she left. Mr. Wallace was planning to drive out to Cleveland before the Fourth of July to spend a couple of weeks with his family. Then Bernadette would be alone in the back bedroom of the strange apartment in the strange little town, alone with her son and a pile of cardboard boxes holding all her best clothes for work—she always tried to look her best—and her bouffant wig. She was working the third shift—11:06 P.M. to 7:36 A.M.—and sleeping during the day. The apartment was downtown, upstairs over a store. No yard. No place for the boy to play. No other kids. He stayed inside and played by himself, and when Mr. Wallace went to work, too, on the shift that overlapped Bernadette's, she had no one to care for him. One day he had diarrhea, and it was all white.

On Friday June 30, two days after she moved to Wallace's apartment, Bernadette phoned the Tioga County Department of Social Services and told the secretary that "she couldn't take it anymore" and that "her boy needed foster care." The secretary asked her to come to the office right away and tell her story to a caseworker, who wrote it all down. Bernadette said she "very much wanted foster care," at least until September, when she hoped to be back on her feet. She knew she was "neglecting" her boy. The caseworker suggested day care or a baby-sitter, but Bernadette insisted that baby-sitters don't care for children as well as foster parents do. The caseworker was more concerned about how Bernadette spent her money. "She brings home $119 net per week, yet, she states she is having trouble having enough money for food. YET, she does not pay any rent!!!" the caseworker marveled. She convinced Bernadette to meet with a counselor to learn about budgeting. They did not speak of Herman, but the next day Bernadette took the boy to him. Herman agreed to take care of him until she moved into her house.

Three days later, on Monday, July 3, the child was staying with Herman's friends Georgia Bowman and Horace Porter in Binghamton, but the Tioga County Department of Social Services was trying to find him a baby-sitter. The caseworker explained to one sitter that Mrs. Powell "is having problems but seems nice." Mrs. Powell, she noted in her report, "feels it is very bad for the child at present time" because "she is just in the air." The caseworker stopped by the apartment with information on day care, but no one was at home. She left a note asking Bernadette to phone the office, but Bernadette never did.

Instead Bernadette waited alone in Tom Wallace's apartment for several days. Then she drove to Ithaca, picked up her teenaged friend Michael Thomas, stopped by Herman's apartment in Endicott, and followed him to Bowman and Porter's apartment in Binghamton to see her son. She complained that Herman hadn't combed the boy's hair or washed his feet. He looked scruffy, she said. Later, on Saturday night, she came back alone to take the child away and followed Herman back to his Endicott apartment to collect the boy's things. Then with her child and, for some reason, her ex-husband, she made once again the familiar trip to Ithaca, and there in an anonymous motel room just after the sun came up that Sunday morning, she shot and killed Herman Smith.

## CHAPTER 2

# HERMAN

Herman David Smith, Jr. Date of birth: June 25, 1947. Place of birth: Biloxi, Mississippi. Oldest son of Herman David Smith, Sr., and Beulah Smith. He was by all accounts a personable kid and a promising athlete, and although he was known to the police from "frequent" encounters, he was never charged with a crime. By the time he graduated tardily from M. F. Nichols High School in 1968 at age twenty, he had picked up a way with cars from his mechanic father and a chest full of tattoos of his own devising. (Even his cheek bore a blue cross, the symbol of the "Machuca-mau" gang, crudely and painfully incised with needles and ball-point pen.) He was labeled "Mr. Wonderful" in his high school yearbook, and on the strength of his athletic prowess won a scholarship to Paul Quinn College in Waco, Texas. It was a slow start but a promising one.

Date of death: July 9, 1978. Place of death: Ithaca, New York. Cause of death: gunshot wound inflicted by ex-wife. Herson's Funeral Home of Ithaca sent Herman David Smith, Jr., back to his parents in Biloxi, to the sprawling unpainted frame house just a block off "black main street," the ramshackle bungalow with chickens still strutting the backyard, where as a kid Hermie Jr. had cleaned the fish he caught. After the Tompkins County coroner finished the autopsy, the corpse was in bits and pieces; but the coroner sent the remains over to Herson's, and Herson's shipped them, packed in a tasteful box, to Galloway and Son Funeral Home in Biloxi. On Saturday, July 15, after a service attended by his five brothers and six sisters and many family friends, Herman David Smith, Jr., was buried in the Biloxi Cemetery. He was thirty-one years old.

Only ten years had elapsed since Hermie Smith, known as "Spark," a name that was tattooed by hand on his chest, left home with the blessings of his family and his community to make good. What happened in those ten years is hard to piece together, for Hermie never did make a place for himself, never did live up to the slim promise of his youth in black Biloxi. Instead, in Ralph Ellison's phrase, he "fell out of history."

He went off to Paul Quinn College in September 1968. Perhaps the pressure was too great. Perhaps it baffled him that he was just a freshman and not, as he had been back in Biloxi, "Mr. Wonderful." Perhaps it was just too hard for a down-home boy to be so far from home. Perhaps he missed the girl he left behind. In November he was arrested in Austin for drunk driving, and when the semester ended, just after Christmas, Hermie Smith went home again to Biloxi. There, some said, he had a girl friend and a child whom he did not want to claim. (The girl—the woman—showed up, all those years later, at the funeral.) But in February Hermie left home again to try his luck in the north.

He went to Endicott, New York, to the home of Everett and Eloise Jackson, old family friends, good folks with five sons of their own, dedicated to giving to black kids in trouble a break they wouldn't get from the white world. Eloise Jackson taught school, and Everett Jackson, who had a good job at IBM, was an officer of the local NAACP. Together over the years they cared for a long succession of foster children, and they offered to take Hermie in as their own.

It didn't work out. Within six weeks he moved to Binghamton, to a run-down hotel on Susquehanna Street, the heart of the ghetto. That's where he was living when he was arrested on April 26, 1969, for breaking into Irving's Market to help himself to some beer he said he needed to take to his girl friend's and would have bought had the store been open. As a matter of fact, he helped himself to the makings of a party: seven ice-cold six-packs, some ginger ale and Dixie cups, thirty-three packs of cigarettes, five William Penn cigars, a box of matches, eleven bags of Wise's Bacon Delites, and a transistor radio. And as though he knew that all parties must end, he also grabbed an alarm clock, a bottle of aspirin, a package of Alka-Seltzer, and six bottles and cans of black shoe polish. He didn't name his girl friend, but he did give the police the name of his common-law wife, Jancis Kemp, and acknowledged that he had one child. Whether Jancis Kemp was in Biloxi or Binghamton wasn't clear. The police officially recorded him as a single man—and an impulsive one. They fingerprinted him and photographed him wearing a goatee, a natty plaid jacket, and the number 7519. They charged him with burglary in the third degree, a class-D felony, to which he pleaded not guilty. And because he could not come up with two thousand dollars in cash for bail, they sent him to the Broome County Jail until May 5, when the Grand Jury indicted him. Arraigned again in September, he pleaded guilty and was placed on probation for five years.

A year later, in August 1970, he was arrested again, this time for shooting at a black man named Frank Davis with a .22-caliber revolver made by R.G. Industries—the same sort of weapon with which he in turn was shot by Bernadette Powell. Smith also used the gun to pistol-whip Davis, so that when the police found Davis standing in the middle of Susquehanna Street in front of the Open Door Tavern, he was "bleeding profusely" from the head. Smith himself was lying unconscious on the pavement, for Davis had struck back with a pool cue. Both men had to be hospitalized. Davis, who did not remember seeing Smith before, said Smith told him he was angry because Davis had thrown Smith out of his house "some time ago." Smith told police that before his fight with Davis he had gone to a wedding and had a lot to drink. After that he remembered nothing at all.

Charged with assault in the third degree, a class-A misdemeanor, Smith pleaded not guilty and was released in his own custody. Arraigned again for possession of a weapon, a class-D felony, he was again sent to Broome County Jail for a short time, awaiting action—which the Grand Jury never took—and then released. If Smith was a public danger, he seemed to be so only on Susquehanna Street. And besides, to the men of the whites-only police force, who found the general run of Susquehanna Street blacks abrasive and hostile, Smith seemed different. He was soft-spoken, affable, even deferential—too impulsive by far, but no hoodlum, and certainly no black-power agitator.

Lanky, good-looking, easygoing, Hermie Smith was noticed as the new guy in town, different from the other guys who hung around Columbus Park swigging out of brown paper bags. He worked at odd jobs—laborer, painter, maintenance man—and pretty regularly at that. He kept a little to himself. He was good-humored, polite, and no big talker. Women could see that he was different in some ways that mattered. But by that time Hermie had met Bernadette Alyce Powell at a Susquehanna Street beer bar where nobody particularly noticed the customers' ages. Little Bernie Powell was just sixteen, brimming with high spirits and fun, yet proud and more than a little disdainful of those who weren't quite up to her standards. She was a snappy dresser, dolling up in outfits of perfectly ordinary clothes combined in ways that would have occurred to no one else. Like Bernie herself, Hermie believed that she was "different." For two young people who came from ghettos—one in Biloxi, one in Binghamton—"different" was important, for different meant "better," and better meant a way out, a way up.

Bernadette and Herman ran into each other from time to time in that bar on Susquehanna Street. He wanted to take her out, show her a good time, but her mother thought she was too young to be dating. So they didn't go out; they just ran into each other. He used to wait for her outside North High and walk her home, or almost home. He used to pick her up as she walked to school in the morning. Then she went to his rooming house. By the fall of 1969 Bernadette knew she was pregnant. Herman was pleased and proud of himself. He told everyone about it and said he would marry Bernadette. But her mother sent her away. When she came back from Utica, he was waiting for her, and when she left him again to go to school in Rochester, he followed her. At last he persuaded her to run away with him, and in April 1971 they were married by a magistrate in Montrose, Pennsylvania.

Ten months later their son, the one they would keep, was born at a Binghamton hospital. And in the fall Herman, as good as his word, bought Bernadette her dream house. It was a modest twenty-thousand-dollar, single-story three-bedroom tract house in a subdivision outside the village of Vestal Center. Bernie had the same snazzy way with interior decoration that she had with her wardrobe, and Herman watched proudly as she filled the little house with yellow vinyl couches and glass-topped tables and chrome chairs and white simulated-fur rugs. After all, it was Herman who had dreamed this dream more insistently than Bernadette, who would have been, if she could, a business executive.

It was Herman who built along the back property line the fence of decorative masonry blocks. It was Herman who erected along the side and front of the corner lot the stockade fence to shield their picture window from the neighbors' picture windows just across the street. It was Herman who built the stone and masonry columns on the front of the frame house to give it what Bernadette called a "Spanish influence," Herman who supervised installation of the wrought-iron "Spanish" gate Bernadette ordered for the driveway, Herman who built in the backyard a barbecue pit of concrete blocks. It was Herman who painted the house and mowed the lawn and washed the two cars and then went to work at his shop in Binghamton, where in 1973 he began doing business as Southern Tier Auto Reconditioning and Used Cars.

At night he came home and played with the baby and sat on a chrome chair at the glass-topped dining table and ate the dinner Bernadette cooked and then watched television and drank beer in the back bedroom, which Bernadette had fixed over as a TV room. (Herman himself built the book-cases, which held not books but the second color television set; and he built the raised platform where his own vinyl TV chair stood, important and lonely as a throne.) Then they went to bed, and if Bernadette was in the mood they made love. If she wasn't, well, with the wine and beer he'd put away at work and during the evening, he was ready to go off to sleep. In the morning he would be up early to get to the garage in Binghamton on time. All day, working on cars and sipping Ripple, he knew that Bernadette was at home in the "Spanish-influenced" tract house cooking his dinner, taking care of his son, polishing the glass tables with Windex. This was his dream and he achieved it. This, he knew, should make him happy.

Somehow it did not. And his discontent showed up on the blotter of the Vestal Police Department. Herman David Smith, Jr.—new husband, new father, new homeowner, new businessman—began to beat his wife. Soon there wasn't a cop in town who didn't know where the Smith residence was. Between the day in 1973 when she first called the police and 1977 when at last the troubled Smiths broke up and moved away, the Vestal Police recorded nineteen "cases involving Herman D. Smith, Jr., of 112 Tharp Street."

The trouble was that it cost so much to maintain the dream: to keep up the payments on the house and the furniture and the cars and all the clothes that Bernadette liked to buy for herself and the boy, and to pay the rent on the shop and even just to keep the old refrigerator at the shop stocked with the sweet wine he liked to sip and offer around to his friends who stopped by. To tell the truth, the business wasn't doing all that well. Herman was good with cars, all right. Everyone said that. He'd worked out an arrangement with the Chevy dealer to spruce up all the used cars he took in. Herman would go up there and pick up a car and take it down to his shop on Front Street and open a bottle of wine and get to work. But there just wasn't that much call for auto reconditioning. Business was especially slow during the winter, and winters are long in upstate New York.

What was an unskilled black man to do—or a skilled one, for that matter? Dreaming the American dream, Herman went ahead and bought his suburban home, but it hurt him that happiness did not leach down through the wallpaper. It dismayed him that although he and Bernadette shared the dream, it seemed to be up to him, solely up to him, to pay for it. And it baffled him completely that although he worked hard all the time, he could not meet the bills. He got to drinking fairly steadily all day long, never really drunk, never really sober, so he didn't have to think about it too much. For when he did think about it, he knew, in his worst moments, that he would not measure up to his own life.

He worked as hard as he could, but when he gave Bernadette the money for housekeeping, it just seemed to disappear. There was never any food in the house anymore, and he always had to pick up the beer himself on the way home. He couldn't understand it, until he figured out that her family must be eating the food. Probably they came by during the day when he was at work and ate up everything they could find. He knew her brother, Oscar Lee, must be drinking the beer. Bernadette denied it and told him that things were just the other way around: she had taken to stopping by her mother's apartment in Binghamton about lunchtime, just to get some food for herself and the boy. If Herman didn't get some money soon, she said, they'd starve. What kind of a man was he anyway, who couldn't even feed his child? And him always running on about having more children.

That kind of talk hurt. And it hurt too when Bernadette got herself a job as a Pinkerton guard. She said she only wanted to help out, and the job only lasted a month, but still it looked bad. Herman didn't want her to work. That wasn't part of the dream. He wanted her to stay home and look after the house and the boy and him. He wanted things to be the way they were, or at least the way he thought they were going to be when they first moved in to Tharp Street and Bernadette ordered all those mirrors installed on the living-room wall. That was nice. That was the good time.

He let the business slide and got a job at the GAF plant working the line making film. He was only the third black man they'd hired, but he didn't run into any problems. His friend Horace Porter always was seeing racism here and there, but Herman just let things ride by and he didn't have trouble. The work and the pay were steady, and in his off-hours he could still work at the auto shop and hustle odd lots of goods that came in the way of a man who was always looking to make a buck. He sold things out of his locker at work to the other guys in the plant—dishes and pots and pans and electrical appliances, stuff like that—and even when the foreman asked him to cut it out, Herman could tell that the man admired his enterprise.

He brought money home on a regular basis, but it didn't seem to cover everything. Bernadette got a job at GAF, too, and although Herman had to admit they needed the second paycheck, he still didn't like the idea of his wife going to work in a plant with other men. She was too attractive and still a good dresser, a real knockout, he thought. Every now and again some girl Herman knew and ran into in the clubs would drop by the auto shop just to say hello, and they'd find their way to the little apartment he kept above the garage. It was just a good-time quickie to him, but if Bernadette was out working with other men, how could he be sure she wouldn't do the same thing? He'd slept with enough married women himself to know they liked to slip around. Just the thought of it made him crazy. Some other man and his little Bernadette. He wanted more than anything to have more kids, but if Bernadette went on working, how would he know for sure that the kids were *his*? They fought about it, and about his women too, again and again. He hit her more often and harder. He came home from work one day to find his best clothes burning in the barbecue pit.

Just about a year after Bernadette Smith first went to court for an order of protection, she became pregnant again; and in July 1975 she had an abortion. She says now that Herman insisted upon it, claiming he didn't know who the father was.

But what was the point of the whole thing—the hard work, the payments, the picture window, and the Spanish gate—if there were not to be children? A dream with no posterity was no dream at all, but a whimsy. In October, Herman, who had been ordered repeatedly by the court to keep away from his own home, his own wife and child, went home anyway and beat Bernadette badly. The next day he went home again and found Bernadette and Oscar Lee sitting on his sofa drinking his beer listening to his stereo. He took the place apart. It took less than five minutes, all told, to turn everything he had worked for in the last two years, everything he had dreamed about for years before, to trash. Later, when he and the policeman struggling to arrest him hit the pavement and he felt the cop's ribs give under him, he didn't care what they did to him.

Still the marriage continued, no simple collision of incompatible people but an ongoing disaster. He was dragged along after the crash. Thrown out of his own house by the court, he'd go to a Susquehanna Street hotel until Bernadette felt sorry for him or got lonely or needed some money. Then they'd get together and it would start all over, and then the police would come and he'd wind up in court again. Twice he mixed it up with the cops and they nailed him for resisting arrest. Bernadette filed for divorce, but they made up and tried again. Then she filed again. He was making some money, but too late, and it had come too hard.

In May 1977, he was arrested in Binghamton for drunk driving. That was all he needed. When they looked at his record he'd probably lose his license, maybe even get fined on top of it. How was he supposed to run an auto business without a driver's license? And at the same time the family court was after him to support his kid. What did they want from him anyway?

He wanted to see his son, to take him fishing, but when he caught up with Bernadette a couple days later to ask her about it she was in the bar at the Ramada Inn drinking with some damn people he didn't even know, and he just pulled her up out of her chair and started swatting her, right there in front of everybody. She broke away running, and a couple of security men hustled him out the door. Later, after he'd had a few more drinks, he hooked up with a couple of white girls he knew and went over to the Cadillac Lounge. There, up in the control booth with brother Oscar Lee, the regular DJ, was Bernadette. He asked her to step out in the hall and talk to him, but what he felt he really wanted to do was just pound and pound and pound with both fists as hard as he could on that goddamn fancy wig of hers. So that's what he did. But Oscar Lee was out of the control booth in a second. The two of them had mixed it up before, but this time they were all over the bar, and just about everybody who couldn't get out of the way fast enough threw a few punches. Somebody even stuck a knife in Herman's back. He got out of there somehow and almost made it to his car before the cops caught up with him and took him to the hospital. He told the police he didn't know who stabbed him, but later, when they questioned Bernadette, she said he'd been stabbed by one of the women he came in with.

In July 1977 the divorce was granted to Bernadette. Herman signed over the house to her—it was all he had to give his son—and left Susquehanna Street for the Town House Motel in nearby Endicott. There he lived for six months upstairs in room 23—twin beds, cable TV, and a fridge for beer, but no hot plate allowed—at forty dollars per week.

He was a nice quiet fellow who never caused any trouble, and until the last couple of months or so, paid his rent on time. There Herman Smith started a new life.

He was still working with Horace Porter at GAF, but he also picked up an after-hours job reconditioning cars in Endicott for a guy named Spanky. At the garage he got to know a kid who hung around the place, a white guy almost ten years younger named Dennis. They started going to the bars together, especially to Wapple's in Endicott not far from the Town House Motel, and Hermie met some of Dennis's friends—Jimmy Rollo, Jim English, Fred Schuster, Bob Longo. All of them were young. All of them were white. And though as a rule they didn't get along well with blacks, they all thought Hermie was different, a whole lot more friendly and easygoing. Not that he didn't know his way around. Hermie, who often embellished his plain history, told them about that time he'd been stabbed in a fight at the Cadillac Lounge. He'd walked in one night, he said, and two guys who took him for someone else worked him over and knifed him. He'd had to get a gun and go back and shoot one of them. He hinted that he might have done some time in jail for that little escapade.

In January 1978, Spanky Harrington, Herman's employer at the body shop, offered him a small garage apartment on West Wendall Street in exchange for some help on renovation. Hermie helped remodel the apartment next door, and then, thinking of his friends, and his friends' friends, he started building beds in his own small rooms. He made a double bed out of some plastic tubes he got at the plant and a whole lot of plastic foam. Then he started on double bunks. He built stirrups into the lower bunk, foot blocks at the end of the upper bunk, and he covered the whole structure with shag carpet, except for the underside of the upper bunk, where he fixed a large mirror and some lights hooked up to a timer so they flashed on and off. On the ceiling over the upper bunk he fixed another big mirror. On a sheet he painted a naked woman, like the tattoo carved into his own chest, and suspended it from the ceiling so it could be let down to curtain both bunks, the painted lady's tits in the upper berth and her ass down below. Hermie left the Town House Motel owing the manager $280. He stopped by a couple of times to pay ten bucks on account—which is more than most guys who skipped out ever did—but before long, what with work and one thing and another to do at his new apartment, Hermie let it slide.

Hermie's new friends agreed that the apartment was great. Dennis and Jimmy started sleeping there two or three nights a week. Jimmy was working off and on as a waiter, and Dennis was mostly unemployed, so they had plenty of time to spend at the bars and at Hermie's. They and one or two others—Fred and Jim English mostly—were the regulars. You could count on two or three girls being there, though hardly any of them were there more than a few times. Most of the girls were young teenagers and many had stories to tell, like Kim, who ran away from home because her step-father raped her and was forcing her to bed down with his friends at twenty bucks a roll, which he kept. She was about fourteen, and Hermie was much nicer to her than her step-father, though when it came right down to it, just like Daddy, he turned her over to his friends.

There were so many girls like that, and Hermie seemed to have such a touch with them. He never had to hit them the way some of the younger guys did. Like Hermie, Fred always had some money-making scheme going, and the two of them started talking about opening a house, maybe up in the Syracuse area, where Fred worked during the week. With Fred running the business end of things and Hermie running the girls, they were sure to make a bundle. Hermie told his pals he had "contacts" in Binghamton prostitution, and sure enough, he took them to a black bar where a couple of pimps offered some nice black ladies to the white boys as soon as they walked through the door. Hermie sure knew his way around. Decorating history again, Hermie told them he'd turned his wife out on the street a few times, not so much for the trick money as for the blackmail afterward. Now that's where the big money was.

So Hermie and Fred dreamed, a black pimp's dream, a white capitalist's dream of succulent, pliable female bodies oozing money onto the soiled sheets. In the meantime, they all shared—money, booze, girls. They were good buddies. And mostly they got along just fine because Hermie, as his new friends said, was Hermie. They meant that Hermie wasn't like other black men they knew. In fact, they said, meaning it, Hermie was almost white. Hermie came to think so, too. When people referred to him as black, he would say, "I'm not black. I'm brown." He had been married, he told some of his new friends, to an Italian girl.

But that was all over, and Hermie's new love was a fifteen-year-old girl called Deedee. Like Bernadette, Deedee was slim and small—petite. Her face was clear and angelic. And she was white. Hermie decided she was an angel indeed, and he treated her like one. But while Hermie adored her, his new pals slammed their feet in the stirrups and fucked her just behind the sumptuous ass of Hermie's hand-painted lady. Hermie had given Jimmy Rollo a key to the apartment so the gang could come and go as they pleased, but when he called home and heard Jimmy tell him that he was busy, along with Dennis and a couple of other guys, fucking Deedee, Hermie stayed away. He would disappear for days at a time to take his son fishing or to hang out with Horace Porter and Earl Andrews, the other black guys who worked at GAF. He still had that, his black world, but it grew thinner. He hardly ever stopped by to see the Jacksons anymore, and he tried to stay away from Bernadette. His black friends didn't know he ran with a crowd of white teenagers. His white friends didn't know he had black friends; he told them he didn't much like blacks, especially black women.

Herman Smith spent the last year of his life in this schizoid way. His black friends and his white friends met after his death at the state police barracks.

On Friday night, June 23, 1978, after the bars closed,

Hermie and three of his young friends went back to his place with three eighteen-year-old white girls. They were still there, slouched against the carpeted walls, some of them still drunk, when Bernadette Powell walked in with her little boy at a quarter to seven in the morning. She went to a pay phone on the corner and called the Endicott Police to report that her ex-husband was having a sex and pot party with a bunch of adolescent white girls. Ten minutes later an Endicott policeman knocked on Hermie's door. He checked the girls' identification, determined that they were of age, and finding no evidence of marijuana, he left.

The following Tuesday, June 27, Bernadette Powell repeated her story to Lieutenant Richard Fanara, a detective with the Endicott Police. She seemed concerned for the welfare of her child, but what interested Fanara was the dope. He did a little checking with the neighbors, who confirmed that young white girls came and went at odd hours, and put Herman's apartment under surveillance. On Thursday night and Friday night and all through the following week, the first week in July, Lieutenant Fanara stood in the neighbor's yard and peered over the fence, but Herman Smith never did show up.

Those last weeks of his life were the worst, and they were so bad that when Hermie said he was going to die, as he did to all his friends, he seemed to some of them to be terrified of death but at the same time aiming for it. He said that his ex-wife had a gun and threatened to kill him. He told Dennis and Horace Porter and his old friend Karen Belcher that Bernadette had picked him up, driven him out in the country, pointed a pistol at him, then fired it past his head through the open window. "She's going to kill me," he said. But at other times he said simply, "I'm going to die." To Dennis and Jimmy he spoke of it in the same manner in which he had spoken before of going back south to visit his family and maybe, if he could take his son with him, start a new life. It was not so much a premonition as a plan.

Dennis and Jimmy both noticed that during that last month

Herman, who had eased back on his drinking, shifting down to beer, moved again into high gear. He threw down the booze faster than ever. He didn't get high; he got quickly, irreversibly drunk. And for the first time with his friends he grew quarrelsome. On Thursday night, July 6, when Dennis and Jimmy ran into him at Wapple's, Dennis started joshing him about Deedee. "What's it like to be in love with a whore?" he wanted to know. And Hermie, who was supposed to laugh, got mad. He stayed mad for two hours, arguing off and on with Dennis as they had never argued before; and then he slammed out of the bar. Worried, Dennis looked for him for two days—at other bars and hangouts, at the apartment, at the houses of other friends—but he never found him, and on the third day, Hermie was dead.

Hermie spent his days, during the last week of his life, with his son and with Horace Porter and Georgia Bowman and their kids. The men took their vacation time and went on picnics and fished with the boys. (Georgia's son Michael was almost the same age as Hermie's boy, and seemed the big brother Hermie's boy had unwittingly lost.) And to Georgia, Herman talked. She was halfway in love with him, and she believed that Herman loved her. Even Horace noticed it. "Well, if I split tomorrow," he said with only an edge of jealousy, "we know who'd take care of you."

But at night Herman left the boy with Georgia and Horace and went to Karen's. For years she had been a friend and sometimes a lover. A young white woman, Karen was no angelic Deedee. She was plain, stocky, divorced from a black man, working as a practical nurse, going to school, doing her best to make a living for herself and her kids. Karen, like Hermie, was soft-spoken in the face of monsters. She knew that against life you could not buy insurance. Years later, when one of her children was badly burned and she spent a year easing her back through intensive therapy, she would say only, "My daughter fell into the fire," as though these things happened to everyone. It was the same tone in which Herman said, "I'm going to die," which explains perhaps why he wanted in those days, which he himself announced to be his last, to be with Karen. She had given him the T-shirt he wore that night at Georgia and Horace's when Bernadette came in clutching a black pocketbook— the orange T-shirt that said KAREN FOR SURE, though of course she knew that nothing is for sure, and she wasn't the least bit surprised to learn later that the T-shirt, the T-shirt in which Hermie left Georgia's house to die, had completely disappeared.

After Hermie was shot, when they heard it on the radio, his friends knew instantly that Bernadette had done it. Hadn't Hermie told them? Didn't they know how that woman had dogged him? He told them about the day he came home from work, came home to his beautiful suburban house, and found Bernadette in bed with some guy. Herman tore the place apart. (To Karen he said that he found his wife in bed with a woman, and tore the place apart.) And then, he said, Bernadette drove him up on Mill Hill and fired her revolver at him, right past his head. Everyone knew that story, and some even improved upon it. Jim English told about the day he'd been driving with Hermie when Hermie's "ex" raced by taking potshots at them. As Jim told it to the girls, it was a narrow escape.

Hermie's friends pondered endlessly the baffling question: Why did Hermie leave Horace's apartment that last night and go with Bernadette? If he knew she had a gun, if she had threatened him and shot at him, why would he go with her? Some thought he was just drunk enough to want to have it out with her once and for all about the boy. (He'd said Bernadette was not a fit mother and he wanted to take his son home to the South.) Horace Porter thought Herman expected trouble from Bernadette and protected his friends by getting her out of their house. (The minute she walked in that night, Horace said, Herman grabbed the bourbon bottle, tipped it up, and drained it.) Dennis thought Hermie just gave up on living. "Underneath the surface," Jimmy Rollo said, "Hermie was always looking for something,

something perfect that he never could get a hold of. Towards the end he just seemed to quit."

"Maybe he just set her up to shoot him," another friend theorized. "Maybe he just made up those stories about how she was threatening him. Maybe he just used her. I hate the bitch, but maybe she was doing him a favor. Who knows? What does it matter? Hermie wanted to die."

# CHAPTER 3

# THE INCIDENT

The truck was orange. Nearly everyone agreed on that—
Bernadette Powell, who owned it; the state policeman who
dusted it for fingerprints; the investigator who held out his
hand to receive the keys Powell fished out of her black
pocketbook. They all said the truck was orange, a 1972
Dodge with a camper canopy over the bed of the pickup
and some leafy woodland scenes stenciled on the side panel.
At that moment, early Sunday morning, July 9, 1978, the
truck was parked at the far end of the parking lot behind
the Holiday Inn on the outskirts of Ithaca, New York. It
was the subject of investigation because three people, a few
hours earlier, had taken a ride in it, and now one of them,
Herman Smith, was dead, and another, Bernadette Powell,
had killed him. That much everyone said. But about how
and why and with what forethought the killing took place,
people eventually disagreed. About the color of the truck
you could be fairly certain, but about very little else.

The truck first pulled in to the Holiday Inn early that
morning, and Herman Smith, wearing a tan cap canted over
his thick, wiry hair, entered the lobby to ask for a room for
two adults and a child. He told the man at the desk, night
auditor Dorlyn Brown, that he would check out later in the
day. Brown collected twenty-five dollars in cash from Smith,
gave him the key to room 253, and stamped the registration

card in the time clock. It was 5:54 A.M. Through the glass doors of the motel Brown could see the pickup parked out front. He told Smith to drive around the building to the back lot and park near the middle entrance.

It must have been after eight o'clock when Brown, passing the switchboard on the way to his desk, noticed a light flashing for room 253. He cut into the line, but there was no one on the other end. When he hung up, the light flashed again, but once more, when he cut in, the line was blank. The board went dark and Brown went into the back office to work. A few minutes later he heard the desk clerk shout from the front desk, "Dorlyn, somebody's been shot in two-fifty-three! Some woman just came up and told me."

Brown caught sight of a woman running across the inn's courtyard toward the rear wing, and he pursued her. When she reached the second floor and pushed the half-open door of room 253, he was right behind her. A wide stripe of morning fell between the curtains, which were only partially closed. On the bed near the window lay the man Brown recognized as Herman Smith. He wore the same bright print sportshirt and pale gray slacks he wore when he checked in, but he had taken off his boots. The soles of his bright blue socks were dirty. He lay on his back on top of the bedcovers, his right arm flung loosely across the bed, his left arm concealed by a corner of the bedspread, which was drawn over his left shoulder to cover most of his torso. Blood smeared the bedspread and an exposed part of his chest. His head rested between the pillows, eyes closed, mouth slightly open as in sleep. The tan cap was still cocked jauntily over one eye. To Brown he appeared to be dead.

"I hope he isn't dead," the woman said. She was standing at the foot of the bed watching the reclining man, as though waiting for him to recover, to wake up and move. Behind her, next to a mumbling television set, stood a little boy staring wide-eyed at the man on the bed.

"I hope he isn't dead," the woman said again.

Brown picked up the phone and told the desk clerk to

send an ambulance and the state police. He asked her for the number of the nearest vacant room, then called the housekeeper to bring a pass key.

"It was an accident," the woman said. The man had kidnapped her and her child and brought them here. When he dozed off she tried to get the gun away from him. "But it went off," she said. "It went off."

She picked up the truck keys and her pocketbook from the dresser, dropped the keys into the pocketbook, took the child's hand, and followed Brown down the hall to room 249 to wait for the police. She said she wanted to telephone her mother in Binghamton, fifty miles away, so Brown showed her how to make a long-distance collect call and left the room to wait in the hall. She seemed to be fairly well composed, he thought, and not at all hysterical. The child had not said a word or cried. He only continued to stare.

At 8:34 A.M. the state police at Varna, a few miles up Highway 13, logged the desk clerk's call reporting a shooting at the Holiday Inn. Investigator James P. Eisenberg reached the motel minutes later. In room 253 Herman Smith still appeared to doze upon the bright bedspread, a cartographic print splashed with garish maps of the seven continents and with his own darkening blood. On the bed near his knees, drifting just off the orange coast of Africa, lay a .22-caliber revolver. Eisenberg called his office for help. He had a homicide on his hands. The medical examiner would have to be notified, and the district attorney of Tompkins County. From this point on, they would be a team. The medical examiner would get the corpse, the detectives would get the killer, and the D.A. would get the case.

At first glance it seemed blessedly simple. The dirtiest homicides, the insoluble ones, were the random acts of violence committed upon strangers by "person or persons unknown." But here was a body in room 253, and just two doors down the hall in room 249 was a woman who admitted pulling the trigger. One official guide for detectives instructs them to search out the particulars of a homicide in this order: *when, where, who, what, how, why.* Eisenberg already knew *when* and *where.* A glance at the body told him *what.* The bloody bedspread and the abandoned gun hinted *how.* To learn *who,* he had only to talk with the woman in room 249. Perhaps she would even tell him *why.*

Her name was Bernadette Powell, she said, and the dead man was her ex-husband. They had been divorced for a year. They were together that night only because of the child, their child. She had gone to fetch her son from a visit to his father. Smith kidnapped them, she said, and only when he fell asleep was she able to grab for the gun, hoping to get herself and the child safely out of the room, out of his reach.

"But he sat up—and I pulled the trigger."

When Joe Joch, the district attorney of Tompkins County, came in, Eisenberg sketched the facts: the woman admitted the shooting, and the victim was dead. It seemed a simple enough case: part frightened woman, part threatening man—part self-defense, part accident. The legal mix would be worked out later in plea bargaining between Powell's attorney and the D.A. Powell had committed homicide, but within that broad category were various degrees of intention, responsibility, guilt, and punishment. The question for the district attorney was not whether she killed Smith but what legal offense she had committed in doing so. When he asked Powell what happened, she told her story again.

Later Eisenberg and Joch took Powell up the road to the state police barracks to be fingerprinted and photographed. In a windowless wood-paneled office, like the inside of a crate, they questioned her again. Joch listened carefully for any confusion, any small contradiction. He had been struck earlier, as they prepared to leave the motel, by one small discordant gesture. Powell asked what would become of her truck, and when Eisenberg told her a trooper would drive it to the police barracks after dusting it for fingerprints, she dug into her black pocketbook and handed over the keys of the vehicle in which she said she had been a passenger against her will. The gesture was so casual, so innocent, that it probably meant nothing; yet it was so transparently thoughtless that it might be the single uncontrived detail, the only loose thread, in an otherwise perfectly fabricated story. On the alert, Joch listened; but Powell's story, as she told it for the fifth or sixth time, remained inflexibly the same. At last, with Eisenberg asking the questions, they wrote it down.

I, BERNADETTE ALYCE POWELL, being duly sworn, depose and say: that I am 26 years old having been born on 3/21/52 and I presently reside at 5 Lake Street, Owego, New York, with my son . . . who is six years old. . . .

Q. This statement is to the facts leading to the facts of how you shot your ex-husband HERMAN D. SMITH at the Holiday Inn in the Village of Lansing this morning, are you willing to tell me about this?

A. Yes.

Q. Are you aware of your constitutional rights as I had advised you of earlier this date?

A. Yes.

Q. When did you first see HERMAN prior to the shooting?

A. I went to the house of my sons babysitter on Edwards Street in the City of Binghamton to pick up my son at about midnight HERMAN was there drinking and gambeling. I told them I wanted my son and got him from the bedroom. HERMAN said he had got a bicycle for him but it was at his apartment in Endicott. HERMAN drove his van to the apartment and I followed him in my truck. Once at the apartment he got the bicycle in his van. I told him to put it in the truck, my truck, but he didn't. He said he would drive me to Ithaca, because he believed I still lived in Ithaca and he would drive my truck. I told him I didn't live in Ithaca anymore and he said "We will see." On the way I told him I lived in Owego, New York but he didn't believe me. I didn't tell him the Lake Street address. He drove my truck, I sat in the middle and my son on the outside.

Q. What happened when you got to Owego, New York?

A. He drove on past and I saw signs for Candor and Ithaca, New York. I repeated to HERMAN that I didn't live in Ithaca and he got a small handgun from in front of his pants and held it in his left hand pointing it in my direction. I didn't say much to him because when I said things in the past he pounded me. I didn't know the roads but we ended up in Elmira, New York.

Q. What happened in Elmira?

A. HERMAN stopped at a taxi stand and asked the man where he could get a room. When he got out of the truck to check for the room he said "Don't get out, you can't run fast enough to get away from a gun." He didn't find a room so he drove to Ithaca, New York.

Q. HERMAN drove the car, excuse me, the truck to Ithaca, where did you go?

A. To 36 Abbott Lane, West Village where I had lived before going to Owego. He looked thru the mail slot to see that I had moved out. He had the gun in his left hand holding it down by the side of his leg. He then drove around and checked the motels looking for a room. We then drove up the hill to the Holiday Inn. He parked out front and went in the lobby and got a room. He told me again that I couldn't run from a bullet again. He got in the truck and moved it around back so we could go to the room. I walked in front while HERMAN and my son walked behind. We went into a room on the second floor. I can't remember the room number.

Q. What happened in the room?

A. HERMAN put my son in the bed, the first bed you come to in the room and I covered him up. We sat in the black plastic chairs and talked. He did most of the talking about when I had him arrested about three weeks ago in the Village of Endicott at his apartment.* He was mad about this and was swinging the gun around. After setting in the chair about ten minutes he pointed the gun at me and told me to get on the bed. He took off his work shoes and got on the bed nearest the window, not the bed my son was on, and put the gun down the front of his pants with the handle sticking out. He got the edge of the spread and flipped it over himself. He rolled over on his right side so he was looking at the middle of the bed. I got on the other side of the bed on my right side facing away from him. HERMAN went to sleep several times but woke up after sleeping for just a couple minutes. The only clothing that he took off was his shoes, I didn't take off any of mine.

Q. What time did you get to the room?

A. I don't know but it was starting to get light outside.

Q. Had the lights been turned on?

A. No, but it was light in the room.

Q. How long did you lay on the bed, and what happened then?

A. About twenty minutes, he was falling asleep but I didn't. After a while I herd him snoring so I knew he was asleep. I rolled over real quiet on my back and reached over with my right hand and got the gun out of the top of his pants. He woke up and started to raise up on his side real fast. I pulled the trigger on the gun while it was real close, about a hands distance from his chest. It was just a pop, not a lot of noise. HERMAN fell back down on the bed and said "Bernadette, you know I love you." His mouth was open and he was making a groaning noise. His eyes were rolled back.

Q. What happened then?

A. I jumped up and put the gun on the bed. Then I ran into the hall and tried to get help. I ran to the front

---

* She reported to the Endicott police that Smith had a marijuana party, but he was not arrested.

office and told them a man had been shot and to please help.

Q. Have you ever seen dead people before?

A. No, only in the movies.

Q. Do you think HERMAN was alive when you ran from the room?

A. Yes, he was breathing and gasping for air.

Q. Bernie, I am going to have you read this statement which consists of two pages. If it is true to the best of your belief and knowledge will you sign it?

A. Yes.

Q. Can you read and write?

A. Yes, I graduated from Binghamton North High School and Rochester Business Institute.

Q. Do you know that swearing to something that is true when in fact it is false that you can be charged with the crime of perjury?

A. Right.

After she signed in her schoolgirl script, the letters slightly shaken, not perfectly rounded, they took her to the courtroom of Justice Spry in Lansing Township, the site of the Holiday Inn, on the outskirts of Ithaca. There, on the afternoon of July 9, 1978, Bernadette Alyce Powell was arraigned for manslaughter in the first degree, an offense contrary to the provisions of section 125.20, subdivision 1, of the New York State Penal Code on a felony complaint brought by Investigator James P. Eisenberg. "A person is guilty of manslaughter in the first degree," the complaint notes, "when with intent to cause serious physical injury to another person, he causes the death of such person or of a third person." Further, "at the aforementioned time and place the defendant Bernadette A. Powell, did with intent to cause serious physical injury shoot Herman Smith with a .22-caliber revolver causing the death of Herman Smith. . . ." Justice Spry ordered Powell held for Grand Jury proceedings and set bail at ten thousand dollars. She was taken that very afternoon to Tompkins County Jail. Her mother collected the child.

The investigation was already under way. At ten o'clock that morning, as Eisenberg and the district attorney listened in room 249 to Powell's account of what she would refer to ever after as "the incident," Dr. Manuel Posso, the medical examiner of Tompkins County, entered room 253, grasped the wrist of Herman Smith, and, finding the pulse gone and the flesh cool, pronounced him dead. Dr. Posso raised Smith's eyelids to observe that the eyeballs had rolled up and back, out of sight. He lifted up the bedspread and opened Smith's bloody shirt to examine the tiny round hole in his chest. He flexed Smith's legs and found them already growing rigid. He rolled Smith over and raised his shirt, looking for the characteristic discoloration of blood under the skin, blood no longer coursing through the body but settling under the pull of gravity; but because Smith's skin was dark brown, Posso couldn't see any discoloration. Nor could he find other wounds. He rolled Smith onto his back again, more or less as he had found him.

Posso had left the motel when Investigator Herbert Weidman arrived at 10:30 A.M. The ID man for troop C of the state police, Weidman was in charge of gathering physical evidence from the scene of the crime. He took a series of black-and-white and Polaroid color photographs, of the unused bathroom, the rumpled bed in which the child had slept, the telephone and an open can of orange soda on the nightstand, two ashtrays full of stubbed-out Salems and a crumpled empty pack beside a Gideon Bible on the lamp table, the gun lying on the bedspread, and finally the bed bearing the body of Herman Smith. He photographed Smith from many angles and took close-ups of his head and of his chest, with the shirt partly buttoned, then opened and pulled back, then removed altogether. He snapped a close-up of the wound smeared with something, presumably blood, which showed up in the black-and-white photos only as a dark smudge. And then apparently he wiped away the smear to take another close-up showing much more clearly the flesh around the wound and the wound itself, a tiny round hole, no more than a quarter inch in diameter, drilled right through the head of a naked woman with enormous breasts tattooed crudely just over Smith's heart.

Weidman dusted the bathroom, the nightstand, the lamp table, and the TV table for fingerprints, then inked Smith's fingers and took a set of his prints for comparison. He took a close look at the bedspread, the shirt, and the wound, checking for powder burns or residue, but he found nothing except a tiny slit beside a buttonhole, a slit that might have been made by a bullet. He turned Smith over again, looking for an exit wound, but like Dr. Posso, he found none. In one plastic evidence bag he folded the bloody shirt, and in another he carefully placed the gun. He went through Smith's pants pockets and found a set of keys.

From the window Weidman photographed the orange truck standing at the far end of the parking lot, then went down to the lot for close-ups. The truck was locked, and when he tried to open it with the keys from Smith's pocket, none of them fit. Using another key, which Eisenberg had given him—the key from Bernadette Powell's purse—he opened the door. He searched the truck unsuccessfully for bullets, dusted the cab for fingerprints, and finally tried all the keys he had in the ignition. The only one that fit was the key from Powell's purse.

Weidman turned the truck over to a trooper who was to drive it to the barracks, gathered his camera and evidence bags, and returned to his office at Sidney. There he dusted the gun for prints and removed a single spent casing, the only shell in the six-shot revolver. He put the casing in a tiny clear plastic evidence box and tagged it. He would send the gun and the casing to the ballistics men at the state crime lab in Albany, but first he had to retrieve the fatal bullet, which apparently still lay in the body. At ten o'clock the next morning he went to the Tompkins County Morgue to observe the autopsy and to claim that last bit of evidence.

In the presence of the D.A., an assistant D.A., Investigator Weidman, and another investigator, Dr. Posso opened Herman Smith's chest and found the pleural cavities and the pericardial sac covering the heart filled with blood. He found two holes in the aorta, where the bullet went in and went out, and two holes in the heart, where the bullet went in and went out. Through these holes blood had poured into the chest cavity. As the official cause of death Posso cited "exsanguination inside the chest due to a gunshot wound in the chest." He estimated that the death by exsanguination was "quick," perhaps taking "seconds or very few minutes." Swiftly Herman Smith had bled to death, inside.

From the heart Posso extracted two samples of blood to send to the state crime lab and the Binghamton General Hospital for alcohol-content analysis. Then he went after the bullet, which he had already located on X rays, lodged in the spine. He followed the path to where it lay, wedged into the eighth thoracic vertebra, but he couldn't get it out. With a small electric saw he split open the vertebra and freed the bullet, just knicking it with the blade, and turned it over to Investigator Weidman. It was a .22 caliber, badly deformed by its disastrous journey through Herman Smith.

Posso carefully documented his work using a Polaroid camera with color film. Before opening Smith's chest, he cleaned the wound and photographed the hole, close up. Then he took a shot of the perforated heart lying in the bloody chest cavity. He removed the heart and had his assistant, wearing opaque white rubber gloves, hold it up so the holes were visible to the camera. He photographed the perforated aorta and the vertebra with the stubborn bullet stuck fast. Finally he took a photo of the general chest area, a kind of aerial shot of the bloody terrain, with the rib cage, neatly severed by the electric saw, folded back out of the way, as white and regular as a rack of lamb.

While the specialists, Investigator Weidman and Dr. Posso, dusted and sliced and snapped photographs, other police investigators fanned out from troop-C headquarters at Varna for the routine background investigation. "The best thing about the state police structure," Investigator Eisenberg says, "is the large number of men we can muster under one command on any particular problem." He refers to the state police practice of following identical procedures at every station so that troopers and investigators become interchangeable parts in a big machine, moving as needed from one base to another, slipping easily into the operation. "We can bring in just as much manpower as we need. If we're on to something, we can bring in men from Sidney or Oneonta. You name it." And in the case of Bernadette Powell, as one thing led to another, that is exactly what they did. From Ithaca to Elmira and Binghamton and Endicott, the limitless manpower went to work.

They started with the victim. From the Holiday Inn registration card the police took his address. Endicott, New York, is a small city some thirty-five miles south of Ithaca, a blue-collar community that grew up around the Endicott Johnson Shoe Company. Most of the town straggles out along the Susquehanna River valley following the highway, U.S. 20, as if it were on its way to someplace else. A few streets amble up the bordering hills to "view property," where the lots are a little bigger and the houses newer, but most of Endicott lies in the flats, convenient and not ambitious. On West Wendall Street, the address Herman Smith listed on the motel registration card, the police found the apartment with the strange decor, which one of them described as "basic early pimp." They turned up no guns, no bullets, no dope, only pornographic magazines and the fact that Smith's phone was listed under another name—James Rollo. It didn't take long to learn that Smith had left behind him in Binghamton an unpaid phone bill large enough to have kept him from getting another phone, and to turn up not one but two James Rollos.

The one they wanted was junior, a twenty-year-old waiter who lived most of the time with his parents in a small ranch house on the hillside above West Wendall Street, but who acknowledged that he "hung out a lot" at Herman Smith's apartment. Smith was his good friend, he said, a great guy, the kind of guy who, even though he was so much older, always had time for Jimmy Rollo and his pals and the young girls they brought around. When Investigator Crosier talked to him at his parents' house on the very day of the shooting, Jimmy Rollo couldn't say enough about the good-natured friend whom he called "Hermie." He was hurt and angry about Smith's death, and a little guilty. He should have seen it coming. In his written report Investigator Crosier boiled the interview down to a single remarkable sentence: "James Rollo . . . stated he had been a friend to the deceased HERMAN SMITH for a period of one year and . . . that HERMAN SMITH had told him in the early part of June that BERNADETTE POWELL had reportedly threatened HERMAN SMITH with a revolver. . . ."

Others could vouch for the story, Rollo said, and he named more of Herman Smith's young friends. The next morning, Monday, July 10, Investigator Foulke and Senior Investigator McElligott questioned one of them, Herman's "special" girl friend, Diane "Deedee" Wilson, who had just turned sixteen. She signed a statement that said in part that once, according to Herman, his ex-wife had taken him for a ride and pulled a gun on him. She had also heard, she said, that once in a barroom fight his ex-wife stabbed him.

Tracing backward the last hours of Smith's life, the police also knew by Monday morning that on the night of his death he met Bernadette Powell around midnight at a house in Binghamton, not on Edwards Street, as Powell's statement mistakenly said, but on Yager Street. The ground-floor apartment at number 19 was rented by a black man, Horace Porter, who accompanied Investigator Palmer to the state police barracks at Kirkwood and signed a statement about Herman Smith's last hours. Porter had been home with his wife and Herman and a friend named Earl and "a girl named Karen" when Powell walked in, saying she wanted to talk with Herman. After a five-minute conversation, which Porter did not overhear, Herman gathered up his sleeping son and left with Powell. He said to Porter, "I'll see you tomorrow." Just the week before, Porter added, Herman said that his ex-wife had taken him for a ride and pulled a gun on him. She "told Herman that if she couldn't have him, nobody could have him." Herman didn't like to be around his ex-wife, Porter said. She made him "nervous."

Investigator Foulke found the woman Porter referred to as "a girl named Karen," twenty-three-year-old Karen Belcher. She too had heard stories about Bernadette Powell, and she repeated them in her statement. Herman told her that his ex-wife had a gun and sometimes insisted on playing Russian roulette. Once, not long before, she had taken all the bullets but one out of the gun, then pulled the trigger twice. She took him for a ride up on Mill Hill and put a gun to his head, saying that if she couldn't have him, no one could. And once, Herman told Karen, Bernadette stabbed him three times with a pair of scissors in a fight at the Cadillac Lounge.

That evening the Binghamton newspaper reported that Bernadette Powell was charged with manslaughter. She had been abducted by her ex-husband at gunpoint, the paper said, and shot him while trying to seize his gun. That account sent Georgia Bowman to the telephone to call the state police. She had another version of how Herman Smith went to his death; and the next morning, July 11, she gave it to Investigators Foulke and McElligott.

Herman was playing cards at her apartment with Horace Porter and Earl Andrews when the boy from next door came in to say that a lady outside was looking for him. It was one-thirty in the morning, but there she was, Herman's ex-wife. After she talked with him for a few minutes in the living room, Herman said he was going to take his son home and asked Earl to go with him, promising to drop him off at his place, but Earl didn't go. While she was waiting for him to get the boy, Powell confided in Bowman that Herman, still in love, wanted to marry her again. But only a few days before that, Bowman said, on Thursday July 6, Powell had come to her house with a young black man "hollering and yelling" at Herman. Bowman heard her say, "If you don't do what I tell you to do, I'm going to kill you," and "I have a gun and I'm going to kill you." Herman ignored her.

Bowman described Herman Smith as a "NON-violent and easy going" type, but "very nervous" and "scared for his life." He was "afraid that woman . . . was going to come and kill him." Herman had told Bowman that about two weeks before the Fourth of July Powell drove him up to Mill Street and put a gun to his head, saying that "she didn't want him to have nothing or nobody but her, and if she couldn't have him, nobody could." Herman also described a time when Powell put one bullet in a gun, spun the cylinder, put the gun to his head, and pulled the trigger. "I understood it to be Russian roulette," Bowman said, "although he didn't call it that. He called it a 'game.' "

When Investigator Foulke questioned Earl Andrews two days later, Andrews bore out in rough outline the statements of Horace Porter and Georgia Bowman, but he "had been drinking during the evening," he said, and consequently did "not recall the exact conversations that took place. . . ." As an afterthought, he added, "Herman told me a couple of weeks ago, 'That woman is gonna shoot me one day; she's got a gun.' " To the state police investigators it was becoming a familiar refrain.

Still, all these reports of threats and Russian roulette might be only tall tales. Some of them, like Karen Belcher's report that Smith had been stabbed three times by his ex-wife in the Cadillac Lounge, the police knew to be fabrications. (Binghamton police records said he had been stabbed once in a melee and didn't know who did it.) No one but Georgia Bowman claimed to have heard Powell threaten Smith. The others got their stories secondhand from Smith himself. Had he been developing a cover? Suppose he planned to shoot

Powell in that motel room and claim that *she* abducted *him*? All these witnesses were conveniently primed to corroborate his story that for weeks she had been threatening him with a gun. The setup theory was at least as plausible as any other; and in any event, none of these secondhand tales— all hearsay evidence—could be used in court. If the police were going to challenge Powell's account, they would need more than Herman Smith's stories. But those stories, repeated by his friends, were enough to keep them looking.

They looked in Ithaca where, Powell said, she and her child lived for several months before she moved in June to Owego to be closer to her new job at IBM. They looked in the West Village housing project and in the centers of black social life and information in Ithaca—the Elks Club and, just across the street, the apartment rented by Ralph Brown, who, when he was not at the Elks himself, often had a few friends in the back playing cards. When there was any trouble in the black community in Ithaca, if you wanted to know what was going down, that's where you went. The police dropped by Brown's apartment and the Elks the day after the shooting.

Whether they learned anything or not is hard to say, for the official investigative report, the composite picture drawn by all that police manpower, is a guarded document read only by the police themselves and the prosecutor. Even a defendant's attorney may not be allowed to see the full report. Why this should be so is not clear. Defense attorneys maintain that defendants are entitled to know the full extent of accusations against them and who their accusers are, but police argue that they must protect their sources so that informants will feel safe in cooperating with the police, and so that innocent citizens interviewed will not be tarnished as suspects. So who told the police what and when remains an official secret. Yet almost everyone confronted by the state police cooperates, and even those who think they are not cooperating may, by denial or silence, inadvertently re-

veal something of value. "Everyone's an informant," Jim
Eisenberg says. "Even saying nothing says something."

On Wednesday, July 12, as the investigation continued,
a hearing was held before Justice Spry to set bail on Powell's
manslaughter charge. Despite his uneasiness, District Attorney Joch was impressed by Powell's cooperation, and in
fairness he had to acknowledge that her circumstances made
her a good risk to appear for trial. So it was Joch who argued
that Powell seemed to merit release without the ten thousand
dollars bail Spry had set at her arraignment three days earlier. He pointed out that Powell was tied to the area by
strong family bonds. She had a good job at the IBM plant
in Owego, not far away, and a six-year-old son. "She appears to be very anxious to clear her name and testify before
the Grand Jury," Joch added. Justice Spry ordered Powell
released on her own recognizance. It was all over in ten
minutes, and Powell returned to her mother's house in
Binghamton.

The Ithaca *Journal* printed an account of the hearing
headlined POWELL RELEASED WITHOUT BAIL, and the next
morning, Friday, July 14, at 6:55, Joch answered a phone
call at his home from a woman who did not give her name.
He guessed that she was middle-aged and black. "You better
check out that Bernadette Powell," she said. She had a long
story to tell—different from Powell's—and she named names.
She knew Powell, she said, and she knew that Powell had
planned for months to kill her husband. Powell had bought
a gun, a .22-caliber revolver, from a man named Al Smith,
and during the transaction, which the caller said had taken
place in the West Village apartment of a woman named
Diane Nelson, the gun accidentally went off. Later Powell
practiced firing it in the woods.

At that time the only people who knew that Herman
Smith had been shot with a .22-caliber revolver were the
medical examiner, the investigating officers, the arraigning
judge, the D.A., and his unidentified caller. Impressed, Joch

reported the call to the state police, and the next morning they went to Diane Nelson's apartment with a search warrant. In an ashtray they found a joint and held it up to Nelson just to let her know who had the power there.

"Now don't you run those games on me," she said. "That little bitty weed isn't gonna do you one damn bit of good. But I'm starting to feel like I'm gonna need it." She curled up on the couch, where she had been sleeping, and tried to pretend the police were not going through her dresser. In the bottom drawer, the one she said Powell used while she stayed there, they found a spent shell casing, .22 caliber. They asked Nelson to dress and accompany them to the state police barracks to give them a written statement.

"No way," she said. "I got to go to a wedding."

She went instead to Varna, to the state police barracks, and there she saw several familiar faces—David Brown, Lisa Johnson, Al Smith. "Oh shit!" she said. This wasn't the first time. She had been caught in these set-ups before when somebody else did something illegal in her apartment and she wound up in the police station. "Oh shit!" She knew what was coming next.

I DIANE NELSON HAVING BEEN BORN JANUARY 19, 1955 . . . deposes and says as follows . . . I have known BERNADETTE POWELL since September of 1977 we have been friends since that date. On June 25th, 1978 BERNADETTE came to my apartment and told me that she had been at her husbands apartment in Endicott, New York, her husbands name is HERMAN SMITH and that she was there on the 24th of June and she was mad at her husband because while she was there there was a whole bunch of people sitting around smoking dope and dropping pills and her husband knew that she was bringing their son there to visit him. BERNADETTE said "I'm going to kill that motherfucker." During the time I have known BERNADETTE she has told me she wanted to buy a gun because she might have to shoot her husband, she has mentioned this several times. The day after I came home from the hospital which I think was June 26th, 1978 BERNADETTE was at my apartment and she had been staying with me for about a month and she had been sleeping in my bedroom and she also kept her personal belonging in my bedroom. On this day AL SMITH came to my apartment and he and BERNADETTE went into my bedroom, a few minutes later I heard a lound noise and in my own mind I thought it was a gunshot. I got pissed and I yelled at BERNADETTE. BERNADETTE came out of the bedroom and said the noise was just a cap and DAVID BROWN who was also at my apartment said the same thing. . . . I think later that day BERNADETTE told me she had a gun and that it was in her refrigerator at her apartment in West Village and she also said she had some bullets. BERNADETTE didn't tell where she got the gun from but she said that a friend had got her the bullet I never seen the gun or the bullets. . . .

BERNADETTE told me on the 25th of June, 1978 that she would go see a PSYCHIATRIST because I told he she should always was saying how she wanted to do crazy things to her husband, some of the things was that she said she wanted to kill him. . . .

She signed it *Diane Nelson*, 1:20 P.M., July 15, 1978.

That afternoon Lisa Johnson and David Brown signed statements saying they had been in Diane Nelson's apartment when a gun went off in the back bedroom, a gun that Al Smith appeared to be selling to Bernadette Powell. And Al Smith, a thirty-two-year-old black man with a respectable job and a wife and three children, a man with a lot to lose, who already had been interrogated twice, finally signed a statement saying that he sold a .22-caliber revolver to Bernadette Powell. Diane Nelson was driven back to the West Village housing project in a police car, saying to no one in particular all the way, "Oh shit!"

Jim Eisenberg filled out a form over the signature of Joseph Joch, Tompkins County district attorney, to be delivered to Bernadette Powell.

> PLEASE TAKE NOTICE That you have been arrested for the commission of the crime of Murder in the Second Degree, a felony, in the City/Town/Village of Lansing in Tompkins County, New York.

They picked her up that afternoon, and by the evening of July 15, 1978, she was back in Tompkins County Jail, charged with premeditated murder.

# CHAPTER 4

# BARGAINS

Jail takes you out of circulation. In Tompkins County Jail, Bernadette Powell was to spend, off and on, eleven and a half months. She could not come and go. She could not use the telephone. She had to depend upon other people who came to see her. She learned to wait.

She waited first for Dorothy Wager, the stolid painstaking woman whom she had called for years "my lawyer." "You'll have to talk to my lawyer," she would snap at Herman in an argument. Or, "My lawyer will see about that." Dorothy Wager was a specialist in the practice of "matrimonial law," a mislabeled body of jurisprudence that deals mainly with divorce. She dematrimonialized Bernadette Powell. Because Powell kept changing her mind, three years or more elapsed between the day she first wandered into Wager's office in downtown Binghamton and the day they walked out of a Broome County courtroom together, divorce papers in hand. But in the end "my lawyer" had seen to everything.

When Wager heard about the killing, she said, after pausing to reflect, "I'm not astonished." The newspapers reported that Powell shot her ex-husband while trying to get away from him, and no one knew better than Dorothy Wager that Powell had been trying to get away for years. On Wednesday morning, July 12, she drove to Ithaca to visit the ex–Mrs. Smith in Tompkins County Jail. She couldn't represent Powell; her specialty was divorce, not homicide, and her practice was in Binghamton, not Ithaca. But she would help her find someone else. When she left the jail she went around the corner to the Tompkins County Courthouse and walked upstairs to the office of the only lawyer she knew in Ithaca—Joe Joch, the district attorney. From him she got the names of three or four local attorneys who might do a creditable job in a homicide defense. One man on the list—they were all men—had an office just up the street, and he happened to have a little time on his hands when Dorothy Wager walked in the door.

Dirk Galbraith at thirty-two was the youngest partner in Wiggins, Holmberg, Tsapis, and Galbraith, by Ithaca standards a first-rate law firm. He joined the firm in 1974 after graduating from Cornell Law School in 1971 and serving a short stint in the army and a clerkship in the state appellate court. He inscribed his name on the door as a partner three years later. He liked to say that he had practiced law in Ithaca all his professional life, but when Dorothy Wager went to see him in 1978 his professional life was only about five years old. His specialty, he said, stretching a point, was litigation, but he acknowledged that most lawyers in Ithaca might be said to specialize in litigation. There were far too many of them, and scarcely enough work to go around, so they took what they could get, and if they put two or three similar cases together in the space of a year, they called it a specialty. Galbraith had been in court, all right, and he had the voice for it, an effortless stentorian basso, resonant to the back benches, the envy of every attorney in the county. But only once had he tried a case of homicide. That was two years before, and he lost.

Still, that was 100 percent more homicide experience than most Ithaca lawyers could claim, so Dorothy Wager pronounced him competent and took him over to the jail to sit in the narrow yellow cell and listen to Bernadette Powell tell her story. Powell wanted to hire him, and he agreed to take the case. Satisfied, Dorothy Wager drove back to Binghamton and didn't see Powell again until months later at the trial.

Galbraith had a new client with a case that seemed to be eminently defensible. Even in their brief meeting in the jail, Galbraith concluded that Bernie, as he called her, was intelligent, articulate, an "attractive-looking person." Comparing her to other criminal defendants he'd seen in court, he ranked her "near the top in terms of attractiveness as a witness." She would make a good impression on a jury. Certainly he could make those jurors understand the circumstances under which the manslaughter occurred—almost an accident, really.

That was Wednesday. And that very afternoon, persuaded by a sympathetic district attorney that Bernadette Powell could be trusted to appear for trial, Justice Spry freed Galbraith's attractive new client on her own recognizance.

By the end of the week everything had changed. On Saturday the police arrested Powell again and charged her with murder in the second degree. In New York State, murder in the first degree is reserved for the killing of police officers or prison guards. Murder in the second degree doesn't sound quite as bad, but in most cases it is as bad as you can get.

The following Tuesday, July 18, six days after Galbraith met his new client, he appeared with her in Justice Spry's courtroom at a preliminary hearing to determine whether there was enough evidence to hold her over for another hearing before the Grand Jury. (It was the Grand Jury which would decide what crime had been committed and whether the accused should be formally arraigned for that crime and brought to trial.) Bernadette Powell was not expected to give evidence at the preliminary hearing or to defend herself. She had only to listen as the district attorney sketched the state's case against her. It was the first time she, or Galbraith, had heard it.

Opening the hearing Justice Spry read aloud the "information," the formal accusation made on behalf of the people of the state of New York by State Police Investigator James P. Eisenberg. Except for the words *"intentional* shooting," the facts of the accusation matched the facts Galbraith had learned from Powell. But there was one last sentence that didn't match anything he had been told: ". . . the Defendant planned to murder and . . . the .22-calibre gun was purchased by the defendant prior to the killing."

The district attorney presented only three witnesses—the coroner, Diane Nelson, and Investigator Eisenberg. Dr. Posso described Herman Smith's wound and his massive loss of blood, a condition the doctor found "consistent with death." He described the position of the body, "laying on his back" with the bedspread covering "mostly . . . the lower chest and abdomen" but not the wound. He found no "black marks" around the wound or on the shirt, he said, and no holes in the bedspread, which he examined for "ten, fifteen minutes."

The district attorney next called Diane Nelson, Powell's friend and sometime roommate in the West Village housing project. Galbraith, who had run into Nelson in court before, when some of her shady pals were in trouble, thought her an unlikely companion for Powell. The two women seemed to have nothing in common but their age. His client was educated, well spoken, neat, even demure, but Diane Nelson was street-wise and sleazy, brazenly sexy by habit, and some said by trade.

Joch led her through questions he had put to her before, trying to elicit the statements he wanted in evidence, but Nelson kept qualifying her answers, dulling the edge of her accusations, suggesting a more generous view. On the evening of June 25, she said, Bernadette was angry because her ex-husband "had planned on having her son for the weekend and she took him over to him, and he had a whole bunch of people sitting around smoking dope and getting high."

Nelson's testimony upset Powell. She stood up and shouted

at her reluctant accuser. "He never took drugs in front of my son. . . . My husband never took . . ."

Galbraith shouted her down. "Bernadette! You have got to be quiet!" She sat down, clamped her knees together, clasped her hands in her lap, and bowed her head, locking herself into silence. But the outburst jarred. Accused of murder, she had risen screaming to defend not herself but the man she killed.

The district attorney went on. "At the same time, did she tell you she wanted to kill her ex-husband?"

"She said she felt like she could kill him," Nelson answered, and then added, "I would, too, if it had been my son."

"Did she tell you she wanted to buy a gun to shoot her husband?"

"She told me she wanted to buy a gun because she needed it for protection because they argued a lot."

Led by Joch's questions, Nelson acknowledged that there did "come a time" on June 26 "when a black man by the name of Al" and Bernadette went to the back bedroom together, and then Nelson "heard some noise." "But, like I said," she added, "I didn't know if Al was still there or what." She repeated what Powell said to her afterward. "She told me that, don't worry, Al didn't give her no gun . . . because if she needed a gun, she had a gun in the refrigerator. But Al didn't give her a gun."

"She said she had a gun in her refrigerator?"

Nelson backed off again from the force of her own evidence. "She could have been just bullshitting me to calm me down. She knew I was mad, and so she would have told me anything to calm me down." They never again talked about the gun, or about the bullets, which Powell also claimed to have in her refrigerator. "No, after the conversation," Nelson said, "me and Bernadette just cut our whole conversation."

Cross-examining, Galbraith asked her to read aloud from

the statement she gave the State Police on July 15. " 'During the time I had known Bernadette, she had told me she wanted to buy a gun because she might have to shoot her husband. She had mentioned this several times.' " She broke off reading to explain that the police had written this down "because I told them he was harassing her."

"The reason she wanted to buy the gun was because her husband was harassing her?" Galbraith asked.

"He would come and argue with her. I told that to them because he did it at my house."

"They didn't type that down here, did they?" Galbraith observed, scanning her police statement.

"They was typing," Nelson began to explain, then gave it up. "I don't know. Shit. They was just typing. . . ."

Galbraith turned the questioning to Bernadette Powell's threats against her husband. "Now when Bernadette told you about her husband using drugs and dropping pills when their son was there, you said in the statement here she told you, 'I'm going to kill that Motherfucker.' Is that correct?"

"Yes, she was mad."

"Now, have you ever heard other people say that they were going to kill somebody?" Galbraith asked.

"Yeah, I have said it."

"Did you take her seriously when she said that?"

"No. I thought she was just upset."

"This business about having a gun in the refrigerator—"

"I don't know. I didn't see something. I can't say she had something I didn't see. I never seen a gun. I never seen a bullet. . . . I can't say I saw something I didn't see. . . . I didn't see no gun."

"Did you ever look in her refrigerator?"

"She always had food," Nelson observed, eager to change the subject. Powell, she said, "always had a wild mind" and "just said wild stuff," but she concluded flatly, "I never, never seen a gun, period, altogether."

Finally the district attorney brought on Investigator James

P. Eisenberg, who described in his crisp professional manner how he arrived at the Holiday Inn, saw the body, and met Bernadette Powell.

"The first thing she said was, 'Is he alive?' " to which Eisenberg replied, "I do not believe he is."

"I asked her who owned the gun," he continued. "She said that it was her ex-husband's. I asked her if she ever owned a gun. She said no. I asked her if she ever shot a gun. She said no."

At the police barracks, she reenacted the shooting with his unloaded gun, Eisenberg said, and at the moment the gun would have fired, he noted it was "close"—"less than a foot" away from his chest. When he asked Powell at that time to tell him how far away from Herman's chest the gun was when it went off, she stretched out her fingers, "indicating the distance between the fingers of her hand." He took that to be a distance of six or eight inches. Close.

Galbraith conducted a frustrating cross-examination. Eisenberg was the state's witness, a professional witness, and he did not easily give away information to the defense. He had taken pictures at the scene but he hadn't brought them to court. The ID team had conducted the search of the victim's clothing and the room, and Eisenberg didn't have their notes. He hadn't examined the shirt or the bedcovers because he knew the ID team would do that. The statement he prepared for Powell to sign at the police barracks probably didn't contain all she had told him, but the rest was in his notes, and he didn't have his notes with him. He had observed a "reddening of the skin tissue about the [bullet] hole" in Smith's chest, but he was "not qualified to determine if it was a powder burn." Besides, he'd never before seen a powder burn on black skin, and it was "hard to say" if it might look anything like a "powder burn on white skin" (which he had seen) "because there are definite differences in skin color." About the defendant, Bernadette Powell, he said that her "emotional state" seemed after the shooting to be "very stable."

Galbraith summed up. "Well, Your Honor, I think that circumstances described here really describe an accidental shooting. In terms of this alleged death threat or possession of a weapon, we don't have anybody in court who has ever seen this woman with a weapon. She denied that she ever had it. . . . We have here a woman who is married to a violent man. He beat her up on a number of occasions while they were married. They got a divorce and were back together again on this one evening, unfortunately. Most of the circumstances that Miss Powell described in her statement are relatively consistent with the other facts in the case. I suggest that there is no charge of murder in the second degree supported here." For the prosecution, Mr. Joch rested "on the evidence as it was presented. . . ."

Justice Spry, who said he had "listened carefully to the hearing," held the case for the Grand Jury, and Powell was returned to Tompkins County Jail without bail.

Since the local Lansing court had no authority to fix bail in a class-A felony, Galbraith immediately petitioned the Tompkins County Court to fix bail or to release Powell. Then, as one last poke at his deflating hopes, came the news that his client had no money to pay him for her defense. She thought she could come up with a hundred dollars. He helped her fill out an application to the county court requesting that she be assigned a lawyer to be paid by the county. She owned a truck, she said in the application—the orange pickup—and she had a pretty good job at IBM earning $190 a week. But she had no other resources to pay for a lawyer. (As things turned out, the truck was not paid for, and she lost her job.) When Galbraith went into Tompkins County Court on July 24 for a hearing on his bail motion, he discussed the matter with Judge Bruce Dean; but Powell's financial picture was a blur, too confused to be straightened out in a courtroom conference. Judge Dean decided on the spot to appoint Galbraith to represent Powell. (When the trial was over Dean ordered Galbraith paid $2076.39, only two-thirds of the fee he requested for his work—78 hours in court and 104 hours out of court. But Dean added a pat on the back: "Attorney Galbraith is an excellent trial lawyer, and his trial ability was manifest under adverse circumstances. . . . Defendant, Bernadette Powell, was represented by aggressive, dedicated and competent counsel.")

On August 8 the Tompkins County Grand Jury heard testimony in the matter of the death of Herman Smith. Powell did not appear. She wanted a chance to tell her story to the grand jurors, believing she could convince them of her innocence if only she could talk to them; but Galbraith was determined she should not. No judge presides at Grand Jury hearings, and the defendant's lawyer is not admitted. Galbraith did not want his client squaring off alone with the prosecutor before the grand jurors. "It's a fairly automatic procedure anyway," he explained. "If the D.A. wants to present a case, he gets an indictment." In the case of Bernadette Powell, the D.A. got his indictment—for murder in the second degree.

Judge Dean fixed bail at twenty thousand dollars. Barbara and Leslie Fields mortgaged their property, the achievement of a lifetime, and on August 28, they took Powell home to the old farmhouse to await her trial.

Preparing for any trial, the prosecutor is bound by law to disclose to the defense attorney some, but not all, information he plans to use against the defendant. The process of pretrial disclosure can grow complicated and nasty, as attorneys battle to gain information or to keep it from the other side; but in the case of Bernadette Powell, D.A. Joch saw little reason to withhold information from Galbraith. He had a strong case, but a distasteful one. The defendant was a battered woman, the mother of a young child, no career criminal, no threat to society at large. The victim was a troublemaker and no great loss. Besides, the victim was from Endicott and the defendant was a transient; they didn't even live in Tompkins County. Joch had to think about his constituents. He got good press for appointing Tompkins

County's first female assistant D.A. to head a rape-prosecution unit, and his vigorous campaign against drunk drivers was popular with the voters. Why take on what had to be an unpopular murder case? Why not settle the whole business fast without a trial and save the taxpayers some money? He phoned Galbraith and invited him to come take a look at his files.

Galbraith left that meeting convinced that Powell's case was a lost cause. Against the D.A.'s witnesses—Diane Nelson, Al Smith, and others—Powell's story probably wouldn't hold up. Whether her story was *true* did not concern him. The question was: Would a jury believe it? And the answer in Galbraith's mind was no.

But the D.A. was offering a bargain: let Powell plead guilty to manslaughter and take her chances with the judge. Joch couldn't make any promises on the sentence she might get. The punishment at that time prescribed by law for manslaughter could be as much as twenty years, but the minimum sentence required no jail time at all. Joch would argue in court that Powell should serve time in prison—he felt obliged to do that whenever a life was taken—but Galbraith might persuade the judge that the sentence should be light. Certainly in Powell's character and circumstances and previous unblemished record, he had some good cards to play. It seemed likely to Galbraith, taking account of all the mitigating circumstances in this case, that if Powell pleaded guilty to manslaughter she would serve two or three years in prison and spend a couple of years on probation. It was possible that the sentence would be shorter—a year or two. It was even conceivable (though not likely) that Powell would be sentenced to probation and never serve jail time at all. Considering the kind of case Joch could make against her in a murder trial, Galbraith thought it was a generous offer.

Bernadette Powell didn't agree. She was innocent, she said. She wanted to clear her name. She had to think about her son. She wanted the truth to come out so the boy would know that she was innocent. There could be no question.

Galbraith told her about the D.A.'s case, about the mysterious Al Smith who claimed to have sold her the gun. Al Smith could convict her. But she didn't know any Al Smith, she said. Maybe the D.A. was forcing the man to lie, setting her up. Or maybe "Al Smith" was an alias. Maybe the man was someone she actually knew, but under another name, someone who had it in for her. She asked Galbraith to arrange a meeting with this Al Smith so she could see who he was. The answer to the plea bargain was no.

Galbraith met Al Smith at a downtown diner alone, hoping to persuade him to meet with Powell. But Al Smith refused. Why should he meet with her? It wouldn't change what happened. He told Galbraith the outlines of the story Galbraith already knew, and he told it convincingly. True or not, it was going to sound just as plausible as Powell's story, probably more, to any jury. Worried, Galbraith wrote to a private investigator in Elmira and asked him to dig up "any information which might tend to discredit Al's story . . . or might serve as a basis for impeachment of him as a witness." Hoping the investigator would "develop something fruitful," Galbraith authorized him to "expend the sum of $300," the total amount the county allowed an indigent defendant to hire a private investigator. The sides were hopelessly mismatched. A phalanx of county officials and state police investigators and lab experts were assembling the case against Bernadette Powell, but Galbraith's private eye, in three-hundred-dollar's worth of solitary snooping, never developed anything at all.

On September 8 Galbraith filed routine pretrial motions with the court, part of the legal maneuvering to "discover" the case against his client. He asked the court to direct the D.A. to turn over all the state's scientific tests, a complete list of witnesses the D.A. intended to call, along with copies of statements they had already made, and any information the prosecution had gathered that would tend to show Powell's innocence. He also asked the court to prohibit the D.A. from cross-examining Powell at trial about any of her previous "alleged convictions or bad acts." This request is a standard one in New York State courts, where it is known as a Sandoval motion, named for a precedent-setting decision in the New York State Court of Appeals that held that a defendant's past offenses can't be used in court to suggest her guilt, but they can be used to attack her credibility. In other words, a person on trial for robbery can't be questioned about previous robbery convictions, because the jury will tend to think, Once a robber, always a robber. But she can be questioned about a previous perjury conviction, because the information will tend to show not that she is guilty of robbery, but simply that one can't believe everything she says. For Galbraith, Sandoval had taken on particular importance because the D.A had told him informally (and erroneously) that in 1973 Powell was arrested in Binghamton for assaulting Herman Smith in a tavern brawl and later she was arrested for passing a bad check. That's exactly the kind of "prior bad act"—proven or unproven—that can convince a jury of guilt, so Galbraith tried, through the Sandoval motion, to put Powell's past record off limits.

On November 1 Judge Dean issued his decision. He ordered the prosecutor to hand over to the defense the results of all the scientific tests and all exculpatory evidence showing that Herman Smith had owned a gun or threatened Powell. He denied to Galbraith the names of the prosecution witnesses and their statements. In keeping with another principle of New York State law, the Rosario rule, transcripts of their written statements would be turned over to the defense attorney at the trial, one by one, *after* each witness had testified, and Galbraith would have to read fast and think on his feet. On the Sandoval motion, Dean reserved judgment. "The Court will pass on this issue at about time of trial," he wrote. "It may be that if the turbulent nature of Smith is in issue, similar evidence should be admissible as to defendant." As it turned out, Dean never did make a formal ruling on the Sandoval motion, but at some point during the trial, in chambers, off the record, he must have let the lawyers know he wouldn't grant it. When Powell took the witness stand, Joch questioned her doggedly about the prior bad acts he had mentioned to Galbraith, and more besides—and Galbraith did not object.

Conspicuously missing from Galbraith's list of routine pretrial motions was a move to suppress Powell's confession to the police. Since she had given the statement voluntarily after receiving all the proper Miranda warnings, Galbraith thought that no judge would order it excluded. Besides, he reasoned, her confession tended to exonerate her. Leaving Powell's statement on the record, he was stuck with it, even when he ceased to believe it himself. He could think of nothing but to try once more to convince Powell to accept the D.A.'s offer. "Trust me, Bernie," he said when he laid it all out for her again.

But she slumped forward in her chair, wringing her hands, picking mindlessly at the hem of her skirt. "You don't believe me," she said.

Galbraith, in exasperation, suggested she talk to another lawyer for a second opinion, and she did. Richard Stumbar, another graduate of Cornell Law School (class of 1974) had just set up shop with a new partner in the fall of 1978 when Bernadette Powell walked into his office with her mother, her brother Oscar Lee, and her sister. She complained that her attorney was urging her to plead guilty to manslaughter, even though she was completely innocent. Stumbar listened to her story and talked with the district attorney, who showed him Al Smith's statements about the gun sale. Like Galbraith, Stumbar came away from his meeting with Joch thinking that whether Powell's story was true or not, the jury was not going to believe it. He told Powell that with Galbraith she was in good hands; she should follow his advice. That was as close as he felt he could come to telling her that if she went to trial for murder she would be found guilty.

Galbraith did tell her. Again she refused to bargain. She was speaking the truth, she insisted, and the witnesses against her were lying. Galbraith asked her to return to his office with her grandparents, hoping they would help him to influence her. "My judgment is that these other people are going to be believed," he said. "Miss Powell is going to be disbelieved, and she is going to be convicted. Miss Powell is going to go down the river."

Again Miss Powell said, "I'm not guilty."

Stymied, Galbraith went to see Judge Dean. Without discussing the plea bargain, he told the judge simply that he and his client had such a strong difference of opinion that it was "difficult to interact as attorney and client." He thought Miss Powell might want to have another attorney assigned in his place. Judge Dean said he'd talk things over with Powell.

Bruce G. Dean had worked his way through college and Cornell Law School (class of 1940) as the "Middleweight Flash" and practiced law in Ithaca for twenty-five years before he ran in 1970 as a Republican in a Republican county and became Judge Dean. As a lawyer he handled mostly civil cases, and even as a judge he disliked criminal trials because the attorneys always battled over the tiniest technicalities. Before the Powell case, he sat on only three murder cases; but he had heard several rape cases and was often criticized for the light sentences he handed the men convicted. Yet criticism couldn't touch him. "I always know what I have to do," he says, "and I'm not swayed by public opinion." He has the force of a man who believes that his decisions spring full blown from the "law," unprocessed by the fallible human mind, and hence are always right.

Bernadette Powell went alone to see him. Since he no longer remembers the meeting, she is the only witness to what took place between them, just as she is the only witness to what took place between herself and Herman Smith in the Holiday Inn. She told Judge Dean, she says, that she wanted to change her attorney. She didn't fully trust Galbraith because he had come to the case through D.A. Joch's recommendation and he was tying to get her to change her story. She told Judge Dean she would rather have a Binghamton lawyer or Richard Stumbar, but the judge assured her that others were not as good at lawyering as Dirk Galbraith. Dean grew up in Oswego with Galbraith's father and uncle, so he knew all about the Galbraith family. She couldn't do better than young Galbraith.

Besides, Galbraith had done a lot for "her people," Dean said, pulling out documentation—some papers and letters from men who had been defended by Galbraith and said he had done a good job. Since Dean referred to the men as "your people," Powell assumed they were black. She noticed that they all seemed to be in prison.

Near the end of the meeting, when Judge Dean had spoken for nearly an hour, Galbraith came in and offered to step down from the case. But Dean, who had reassured himself, reassured Galbraith. "I think she's satisfied now." She wasn't, she said later, but she was afraid to say no. Dean, a man who projects himself onto the world too vigorously to take much heed of how the world responds, would have been surprised to learn that he had intimidated her. A year after the meeting with Powell, when he still remembered it, he recalled that after their little talk they had been in perfect agreement.

After Powell met with Richard Stumbar and Judge Dean, she determined two things. She was stuck with Galbraith, and she would not bargain. Galbraith was back at square one, but he too made a decision. Since Powell would not be moved, some attorney had to take her case to trial. By that time he had been working on it for four months. He was carrying around in his head odd scraps of information and hunches hard to pass on to another lawyer. Like it or not, this was *his* case. He turned down the D.A.'s offer and prepared to go to trial.

With the case scheduled for March 1979, Galbraith got down to a logistical problem—how to get his client to court on time. She and her son had moved from her grandparents' farm near Johnson City to her mother's apartment in Binghamton—some fifty miles from Ithaca. A late start, heavy traffic, slick roads, a cranky car, could hold her up; but it wouldn't do for her to be late for her own murder trial. Galbraith turned for help to Rebecca Allerton, director of the Tompkins County Task Force on Battered Women.

Shortly after Galbraith was assigned to the case, Allerton and another member of the task force had visited his office to make sure he knew of Powell's history as a battered woman. That issue seemed to be enormously important to the women, though what it had to do with homicide was not so clear to him. At the end of the meeting Allerton handed him a card giving the address and emergency phone number of the task force, and Galbraith made a little joke about it. "Thanks," he said. "I'll give this to my wife next time I beat her up." Allerton, grim-faced, replied, "In our line of work, that's not funny."

The same age as Powell, Rebecca Allerton moved to Ithaca in 1971 from her all-American hometown—Cape Canaveral. She had dropped out of junior college in Florida to come north with her husband, a student at Ithaca College. She stayed on after the marriage broke up, and even after a fire swept away all her possessions and, it seemed, her past. She read an article about battered women, and it troubled her. She had never before heard of wife-beating. She didn't know it was a feminist issue. She didn't really know what a "feminist issue" was, or a "feminist" for that matter. In 1976, when she moved in with Neil Minnis, he told her that his mother was a battered woman.

Allerton rummaged for more information in the libraries at Cornell. She dropped by the police station, the welfare office, the hospital emergency room, always asking questions. Did they ever see any of these battered women, and what did they do to help them? Sure, everyone knew there were a lot of women out there having a hard time. But what was to be done? The women were nobody's responsibility, really, no agency's official business. Then Allerton met some women from the Suicide Prevention hotline who had noticed how many battered women were among the people longing to die. Together they agreed to find them and to help. That was the beginning of the Tompkins County Task Force on Battered Women.

When she read in the Ithaca *Journal* that Bernadette Powell, charged with murdering her ex-husband, had previously obtained orders of protection against him, Allerton went to the jail to see her. Did Powell have friends and family, she asked. Did she have a lawyer? They talked for a few minutes only, leaning against the walls of the cell, but Allerton offered help, and she went next to Galbraith to offer it again.

To Allerton, Powell seemed dazed and frightened and clearly in need of help. But what kind of help? She had a lawyer who was polite to the women from the task force but plainly not eager for their participation. She had a family to lend moral support. But Powell was obsessively concerned that her arrest would cause her to lose all she had recently gained—the IBM job and the house she was arranging to buy, only blocks from IBM, yet backing on to a green lawn sweeping down to the broad Susquehanna River, a paradise for her little boy. Allerton tried to save the dream; but the beefy fellow in IBM personnel explained that Powell had not been with The Company long enough to be "a *real* IBMer," and the realtor reported that the Farmers Home Administration, which was to have provided a federal housing subsidy, had backed out when Powell was arrested. The realtor, who had a daughter just about Powell's age, liked her client so much that she drove to Ithaca to visit her in jail and break the news that the house by the river would never be hers. Yet even after that, when the job and the house were gone, Powell continued to talk endlessly about them. They had been her hope of starting a new life for herself and her son. And because she understood something about new lives, Allerton continued to listen.

After that she visited Powell in the jail two or three times a week. She couldn't stay long because she had a new baby to look after, but the two women became friends of sorts. Gradually they developed a bond that would carry them through the trial and after. They were good at keeping quiet together. When they were baffled or disheartened, they fell silent. When they were together in their silence, things somehow felt better, even when things were not better at all, even when they were very bad indeed.

Galbraith called on Allerton and the task force for help only once—to raise money for bail. So it surprised her that he called again, only days before the trial, in need of a temporary home for Powell in Ithaca. She talked it over with Neil. "We're going to be in court all day," she said, "and then what else will there be to talk about? If she stays here, things could get very heavy."

But "heavy" was something Neil Minnis knew all about. In September 1972 he had returned to his apartment in the Germantown area of Philadelphia to find it filled with police. In the bathroom, jackknifed on the floor, with the cord of an electric toothbrush lashed around her neck, dead, was Laurie Glassmeyer, age twenty-two, the woman he loved and lived with. The police asked him a lot of questions. "I didn't do it," he said, mourning, but they watched him with wary disbelief and asked him more questions. Allerton was with him in Ithaca when the Philadelphia police phoned, in September 1976, to tell him that another man had confessed. After four years he was "in the clear." But no one knew better than Neil Minnis what it feels like to be suspected and accused unjustly.

The next day Allerton called Galbraith and said, "I guess she can stay with us." She thought the trial would be quick. Powell would go into court and tell the truth, and the jury would acquit her. Despite what Galbraith said—and

Stumbar—about the incredibility of her story, Powell insisted, and Allerton believed, that the jury had only to hear it to acquit her. Neil Minnis, who knew that even when you tell the truth you may be disbelieved, was less optimistic.

Powell herself made one last attempt to avoid the trial, not by plea bargaining, but by appealing directly to the district attorney. In February, without consulting Galbraith or Allerton or anyone else, she wrote him a letter, which he did not answer but forwarded to her attorney. The handwriting ran downhill to her tiny signature jammed into the lower right-hand corner of the page.

Dear Sir;

Mr. Galbrath told me that the reason you are persuing the matter as to my murder second charge is because you want to be judge.

Please sir, you have my job with I.B.M. which probably I will never be able to secure mine and my sons future with again. You have the house I was purchasing, my credit, my good name. Do you have to take away from me the most precious of all, my son. To seperate us again for the last time would cause mental instability for him and suicide for me.

To be judge sir is it worth this. I'm Innocent sir. I've suffered truly enough, more than you could know. Mr. Galbraith will get to the bottom of why these people are telling these lies against me sir just give him time.

With all due respect,
*Bernadette Powell*

But early in March the time ran out. Allerton installed Powell in the extra bedroom and helped her pick out what she would wear to court in the morning—a plain woolen skirt of modest length, a turtleneck jersey, and a pullover vest. The shoes that Powell would wear throughout the trial were eminently practical brown oxfords—decent, serious, workaday shoes. (Galbraith had told her to dress as her mother might.) Her hair had grown to shoulder length, and she pressed it into an impeccable pageboy. Around her neck, against the advice of her lawyer, she would wear every day a large silver cross.

# CHAPTER 5

# PROSECUTION

On Wednesday, March 6, 1979, almost eight months to the day after the death of Herman David Smith, Jr., the clerk of Tompkins County Court called the case of *The People of the State of New York* v. *Bernadette Powell*. The court stenographer huddled below the judge's bench, her stenotype machine clutched between her knees like a skinny cello, ready to take it all down. The clerk, Nancy Morgan, a woman of about Powell's age, soon to become the second wife of D.A. Joe Joch, called the names of the first panel of potential jurors, and the lawyers began the *voir dire*, the questioning of candidates to see who would and would not do: "Where do you work? How long have you been in that job? Where did you go to school? Married? Any children?" The first juror sworn, Caesar George, the high school football coach, in seat number four, became the foreman. The clerk called another panel to fill the empty chairs, and the questioning began again.

For the jury Joch wanted good solid citizens, proud of their city and not kindly disposed to outsiders—especially *black* outsiders—who passed through only long enough to bilk welfare and cause trouble. Racism, Joch knew, was bound to be a factor in the trial. Black jurors might sympathize with a black defendant, but in this case, where the victim also was black, black *male* jurors might sympathize with the dead man and be hostile to the defendant. The biases of blacks, Joch thought, would cancel each other out. But white racism was a different story. Before they began even to consider Powell's guilt or innocence, white racists would find her guilty of being black. That in itself would be her crime. In this case, racism could work only to the advantage of the prosecution, so Joch decided that while questioning the potential jurors he would not bring it up.

It was Galbraith who had to raise the issue. The few black people summoned to the panel were quickly excused, mostly for cause, because they knew one or more of the black witnesses who would appear against Bernadette Powell. So one by one Galbraith had to ask the white jurors who re-mained in the box, "Does it make any difference to you that the defendant in this case is black." Some said they were well acquainted with black people. One said that in the service he shared a locker with a black soldier. One after another they replied, some rather indignantly, that the color of the defendant made no difference whatsoever. She could be green or purple or polka-dotted and it wouldn't matter a bit to them. What did he take them for, anyway?

Joch, knowing that Herman Smith was no ideal husband, worried about sympathy flowing to Powell as a woman, a badly battered woman, and as a mother. (The child, the wide-eyed little boy, was in court, seated behind his mother, during the jury selection.) "Just look at the defendant," Joch ordered the potential jurors, "and tell me whether you can tell anything about the guilt or innocence in this case by looking at her. Or by looking at the child." One by one they promised the district attorney they would not find Powell innocent just by looking at her—although all defendants are supposed to be considered innocent until a case against them has been proved. As for Powell's sex, they would be as blind to it as to her color. They vowed to judge the facts only. It would make no difference to them whether the defendant was, as Joch put it, "a woman, a man, or anybody else."

When court adjourned at three o'clock Thursday afternoon, nine men and three women had been seated, along with two women alternates. Most of them met Joe Joch's standard for the ideal juror. They had lived all their lives in Ithaca or one of the surrounding towns—Newfield, North Lansing, Dryden, Trumansburg. Most of their lives they had held the same jobs—office manager, lab technician, telephone installer, data processor, schoolteacher. They had two children or four. They owned their own homes or were paying off the mortgage. Most of them were in their forties or fifties, and at least one was pushing seventy. (The youngest, a woman of Powell's own age, would be the quietest.) By their own account, they were open-minded and not racist. They were fair and had no preformed opinions. All of them were white. Warning them not to listen to the radio, read the newspaper, or discuss the case with anyone, Judge Dean sent them home. The next morning, Friday, March 14, they filed into the jury box promptly at 9:30 to hear the attorneys' opening statements in the trial of Bernadette Powell.

"Okay, ladies and gentlemen, this is the start of the trial now," Joch announced. He told the jurors they would hear testimony about the shooting of Herman Smith from police investigators and experts and from witnesses who either heard Powell make threats against Herman Smith or saw them together that evening. And they would hear "very significant testimony" from a man named Al Smith (no relation to the victim), who sold a gun to Powell. Joch promised to tell the jury what happened the night Herman Smith was killed and what Bernadette Powell had done in the weeks before to prepare for it. This was his case: 1) Bernadette Powell killed Herman Smith, and 2) She had *planned* to kill him.

Galbraith countered that Joch had taken up the story in the wrong place, only a few weeks before Herman's death. "The story goes back a long ways before that," he said. Herman's death was "a combination of a long series of events which began possibly even before the marriage of these parties in 1970." Herman "drank heavily," Galbraith said, and when he drank "he lost his temper and he became prone to commit acts of criminal violence" in the streets and at home. Powell, after years of abuse, divorced him—not because she didn't love him, but because "she was simply afraid of him. She had been afraid throughout her marriage and continued to be afraid of him after the divorce." She went through "hard times" after that and even fell in with some "sleazy people"—black like Powell but totally "unlike her in almost every other way"—who would testify against her. Within a few months Powell "put her life back together," but in "the early morning of July ninth, 1978," when Powell went to pick up her child "after a period of visitation," Herman, "because of his weakness for alcohol, set off a bizarre chain of events which was to end in his death." She *did* shoot Herman, Galbraith conceded, and he recounted Powell's story of that fatal "chain of events." But this evidence, he concluded, "does not amount to the crime of murder."

The jury heard Powell's story again, and much more fully, from the first of the district attorney's long string of witnesses for the state—Investigator Jim Eisenberg. But first, he identified a stack of photos taken at the crime scene and entered into evidence. As the photos slowly passed from hand to hand in the jury box, Herman Smith, a dead man in dirty socks, became for the jurors more than just a name mentioned in a criminal indictment. The gun Eisenberg identified, the gun that appeared in some of the photos, an R.G. 23 six-shot .22-caliber revolver, was tagged as PEOPLE'S EXHIBIT 44. Then, with the preliminaries aside, Eisenberg launched into the story Powell told him about the night of July 8–9, from the moment she arrived at the Bowman-Porter apartment until she ran to the motel desk for help.

When he questioned Powell at the police barracks, Eisenberg said, "she emphatically denied she ever owned a gun, never saw one, never saw Herman with one, never knew how to handle a gun. Her terminology of what a gun was," he added, "didn't even lend to a person knowing about a gun." She referred to the grip as the "handle" and to the muzzle as "the thing where the bullets come out." He asked her to demonstrate for him exactly how the shooting occurred, and as they sat side by side on metal folding chairs at the barracks, she took from him his empty service revolver, drew it across his chest, and pulled the trigger. At the district attorney's request Eisenberg, on the witness stand, pulled out his service revolver, unloaded it, and repeated the demonstration himself, drawing the gun upward from his waist across his chest, and pulling the trigger when the gun was, as he had said, "a hand's distance" from his chest. In the quiet courtroom the firing pin clicked resoundingly on an empty chamber.

After the questioning and the demonstration, Eisenberg said, he took down a statement in writing and Powell signed it. That statement he read aloud to the jurors so that they heard, all over again, Powell's story. Eisenberg almost might have been testifying for the defense, except that Joch began to raise some technical questions with him, some slight discrepancies between that story—told over and over by Bernadette Powell and repeated from the stand over and over by Investigator Eisenberg—and the physical evidence amassed by the experts.

Those technicalities about bullet holes and bedspreads and powder burns—about the distance from which the shot was fired—at first seemed trivial, even beside the point, but in the end they were decisive.

When he examined Herman's shirt at the scene, Eisenberg said, he found what appeared to be a small bullet hole next to one of the buttonholes, but no powder burns. He looked at the bedspread but found nothing unusual about it. He looked at Herman's chest and saw no powder burns. (He did not mention, as he had at the preliminary hearing, the reddened "irregularity" he observed around the wound and thought to be, possibly, a powder burn.) Bit by bit Joch was building the evidence to dispute Powell's story that she fired the gun only "a hand's distance" from Herman's chest. Eisenberg was only the first of Joch's witnesses who found no powder burns on Herman's shirt or chest, indicating that the gun had been fired from much farther away.

Joch asked Eisenberg to look particularly at exhibits 2 and 6, two photographs of the body, to prove that the bedspread could not have been in the line of fire, could not have received the missing powder burns. Eisenberg confirmed that both photos depicted the body as he first saw it, with the bedspread covering only the "hip region" and lower torso, leaving the chest exposed. Neither man seemed to notice, as the jurors too failed to see, that exhibits 2 and 6 were not at all alike. Exhibit 6, taken by state police ID man Herbert Weidman, depicted the body as Eisenberg described it on the stand. But exhibit 2, taken before Investigator Weidman arrived, probably by Eisenberg himself, showed the body apparently as it lay before anyone touched it, even before anyone opened the draperies in the semidarkened room. The upper left-hand corner of the bedspread wrapped over Herman's left shoulder and fell across his body almost to his knees, covering his hips, his lower torso, and his chest.

Like Eisenberg, Dr. Posso, who came next to the witness stand, said he hadn't seen any powder burns on the shirt or the chest. (No one asked him about the bedspread.) He brought along his colorful Polaroid shots of the autopsy, and as he described his procedures, Joch passed the photos to the jurors. Some of them turned away. Others studied the photos hard, as if trying to search out a familiar face or landmark. Some of them found it difficult later to remember that this grisly dismembering had been done by Dr. Posso, not Bernadette Powell.

Because the blood samples Posso drew from the body during the autopsy tested out at only .03 percent alcohol, Posso concluded that Herman was not drunk at the time he died; but on cross-examination he admitted he had never heard of Widmark's formula, by which an earlier blood alcohol level may be calculated from a sample taken at a later time. According to that formula, Galbraith suggested,

Herman's blood alcohol level at midnight on the night of his death would have been nearly 0.16 percent, and at Galbraith's request Dr. Posso read from a medical reference book a list of physiological symptoms occurring at that level: "Loss of muscular coordination, staggering, staggering gait, marked mental confusion, exaggeration of emotions, dizziness, decreased pain response, disorientation, and thickening of speech."

Joch countered by calling Dorlyn Brown, the night auditor of the Holiday Inn, to describe Herman's appearance when he checked in. Brown had seen nothing unusual about the man—no signs of drunkenness, no anxious behavior, no ominous bulges in his clothing. To Brown, Herman seemed sober and calm.

Then, to back up Eisenberg's testimony, Joch handed Brown exhibit 2, the very first photograph, clearly showing the bedspread draped across Herman Smith's shoulder and chest. He asked if that photograph correctly depicted the body as Brown, the first person to reach the scene, first saw it; and surprisingly Brown said no. The bedspread appeared to have been "moved," he said, for when he first saw the body the bedspread was covering the wound even more "completely" than it did in the photograph. Joch suggested that Brown was mistaken, that he had confused the bedspread covering Herman's lower torso with the shirt covering the wound. But Brown was insistent. "I remember the bedspread," he said. "It was keeping me from seeing directly." Galbraith took up the question on cross-examination, asking if it was "fair to say that a corner of the bedspread was covering the left half of the chest?" "Yes, basically," Brown replied. But that was as far as Galbraith could go. He had looked over the state's scientific evidence, but he had given no thought to a bedspread. (Nor would he. The bedspread, a critical bit of physical evidence that disappeared from the crime scene, vanishes from the case.)

Quickly Joch brought another of his experts to the stand— Investigator Weidman of the state police ID squad. At the scene he had performed "a visual check" on "the cover that was laying partially over [the] body" and on the shirt and the skin, he said, but he "observed no gunpowder" at all. But when Galbraith cross-examined him on the growing question of powder burns, Weidman acknowledged that Herman's shirt was "a slippery material" and that while powder residue might stick to the surface, it was also possible that it might not. He wasn't a firearms expert, he said, but he had discussed the matter "telephonically" in July 1978 with an expert from the state police firearms laboratory, Senior Investigator Allen G. Smith, and concluded that it was impossible to tell the distance at which the gun had been fired. The laboratory experts couldn't tell either, or so Weidman testified to the Grand Jury. Galbraith, who according to the Rosario rule had been handed a transcript of that testimony, read part of it back to Weidman—over Joch's objections. "I did discuss this with the laboratory," Weidman had said, but because of the slipperiness of Smith's shirt, "they couldn't testify one way or the other whether or not there was powder burns." A member of the Grand Jury had asked, "In other words, you couldn't tell if [the gun when it fired] was six inches or six feet away?" And Weidman had answered, "Correct."

Galbraith had turned Investigator Weidman's testimony to his own account, but Joch brought on another police expert to attack a different front. The testimony of Fred Hammond, a retired state trooper who had tested the gun, was designed to contradict Powell's statement that it simply "went off." When the revolver was not cocked in advance, Hammond explained, it required "considerable effort to fire" it, an effort of nine and one-half foot pounds of pressure, to be exact. (Galbraith did not challenge the assumption that the gun was not cocked when Powell seized it.) Joch, who was adept at drawing the jurors into the drama, passed the empty gun to them, and each of them in turn pointed it at the floor and exerted nine and one-half foot pounds of pressure on the trigger. Click. Click. Click.

Then, as unheard gunshots, deliberately fired, ricocheted in the jurors' imaginations, Joch called his prize witness— Al Smith. He had known Bernadette Powell more than a year, he said, though he saw her only now and then. One day she asked him if he knew where she could get a gun. Joch showed him people's exhibit 44 and asked if he recognized it. Yes, Al Smith said, it was the .22-caliber revolver his brother-in-law had given him five years earlier. He recognized the engraved model number "R.G. 23" and some peculiar rough marks he'd made once on the front sight in cleaning it. "Did there come a time . . . in the state police barracks when you saw that pistol?" Joch asked, but before he could answer, Bernadette Powell cried out, clapped her hands over her mouth, and ran from the courtroom.

Rebecca Allerton followed Powell to the women's room and found her bending over the toilet bowl heaving dryly, sobbing, and struggling for breath. Her wide eyes were full of tears and panic. Close behind Allerton came Margie Powell, who gripped her daughter's arms, spun her around, and slapped her once, hard and full in the face. "Stop it, Bernadette," she said low and sharp. "Think about your son. Stop it." And Bernadette stopped, or tried to, stifling her sobs, but gasping still for breath. She sat back on the washbasin, leaning into the corner, her face hot and wet, and said over and over, "I don't know who he is. I can't help my attorney. I never saw him before. I can't help my attorney."

Allerton helplessly held her hand, but Margie Powell pulled Bernadette to her feet, shook her again, and said, "You have to go back in there. Think of your son."

In the courtroom Galbraith nonchalantly pulled out his pocket comb and applied it to his long blond hair, as though Powell's headlong flight from this confrontation with the state's star witness were a perfectly humdrum event. Judge Dean was solicitous. Did Mr. Galbraith want to summon a doctor for his client? No, no, that wasn't necessary. Just a little stomach upset. Something she ate, perhaps. Still, Galbraith knew well enough how it looked.

Fifteen minutes later Powell resumed her seat in the courtroom, perfectly poised, as though nothing extraordinary had happened, and Al Smith took the stand again. He said that Bernadette Powell, who had asked him about a gun in the wintertime, asked him again near the end of June, "on a Monday or a Tuesday" or "one of those days," if he was ready to sell his gun yet. He told her he was, for seventy-five dollars. On Friday June 23, he brought it to her at Diane Nelson's apartment, where she was alone, but when she told him she had only fifty dollars, he pocketed the gun and the five bullets he had brought along and prepared to leave. She told him she would get a paycheck on Sunday. On Monday he phoned her at Nelson's apartment, and she told him she had the money. By that time Al Smith was feeling a little guilty because he knew he was overcharging her for the gun. On Friday, when he showed her five bullets, she had said to him, "Is that all the bullets I get for seventy-five dollars?" So after he called her on Monday he stopped off at Weston's discount store and bought a box of fifty .22-short bullets. The purchase, like all ammunition sales at the store, was recorded by the clerk, who entered Al Smith's name and driver's license number in a register. After work, still wearing his mailman's uniform, he went to Diane Nelson's apartment and headed for the back bedroom where Nelson told him he would find Powell. He put the bullets on the dresser, he said—the five .22-long bullets and the new box of .22 shorts—and handed the gun to Powell, who asked him how it worked and started putting bullets in the cylinder.

"What happened then?" Joch asked.

"At first, I was standing in front of her. And, you know, like something just said, Well I better not stand in front of her. And the next thing I knew the gun went off." In the hard cover of an orange book on the dresser a hole appeared, and he opened the book to make sure the bullet had not passed through it. He was afraid, he said, that it might have gone through the wall and struck one of the children he could hear playing on the terrace. He saw the bullet still lodged in the book, and then he left the apartment, walking "real fast," and ran to another apartment, number 50, where one of his girl friends lived. He saw the gun again at the state police barracks, but he didn't know what became of the orange book.

The story was no surprise to Galbraith, but in the months since he first heard it from Al Smith himself in a booth at the Ithaca Diner he had found no evidence to refute it, nothing at all to contradict it except Powell's own denial. If the trial was going to come down to that—to his word against hers—Galbraith had to discredit Al Smith, had to make him look like such a natural-born liar that the jury would never believe him.

Cross-examining, Galbraith questioned him about some of his "difficulties . . . in the past with the police." In 1976, Al admitted, he punched his wife in the face, "requiring her hospitalization." He denied having an affair with Colleen Barnes and choking her, but he acknowledged that he slapped her and chased her husband, "a dope addict," around West Village with a shotgun. No, he said, he didn't break into Joan Phillips's house in 1978. No, he didn't strike her and shove her against the wall. He had never sold handguns before, he said, but he claimed to know "a lot of people" in Ithaca who carried handguns all the time. "What caliber guns are they?" Galbraith asked, and Al Smith defiantly shot back, "You name them, they got them." Nervousness made Al Smith flippant, but even as Galbraith listened to his smart-aleck answers he could see opening before some of the cautious, upright jurors a vision of their quiet town overrun by men like this, strange, dark, jumpy men who carried guns and shot drugs and talked about it all glibly in a lingo hard to understand, men who spent their days down there in the flats gambling in the back rooms of dingy apartments and their nights drinking and brawling and beating up other men's wives as well as their own, breaking in, burglarizing, terrorizing. It was a vision new and terrible of the other Ithaca. Who would want to believe it? Galbraith had only to give Al Smith a motive for lying about Powell, and he found it in the question of immunity from prosecution.

"Isn't it a fact," Galbraith asked, "that after you initially told the state police that you didn't know anything about this incident, the reason that you changed your mind and told them what you did is because they promised you immunity?"

Al Smith denied it, but Galbraith produced a copy of his testimony before the Grand Jury and pursued the issue.

"Mr. Smith, before the Grand Jury, were you asked the following questions and did you give the following answers? 'Question: Tell the Grand Jury how you came to tell the police this information. Answer: The police came to me the first day and asked me had I sold her the gun, and I said no. So then about the end of the week—it was on a Saturday—they came back to me again and they was talking to me. So I just told them. . . . Question: And what was the reason you changed your mind and told them the second time? Answer: Well, they promised me immunity for selling the gun.' Were you asked those questions and did you give those answers?" Galbraith asked.

"Yes."

"And the reason you changed your story was because they gave you immunity, wasn't it?"

"No."

Galbraith, who thought he knew when he was ahead, said, "No further questions," and sat down, leaving Al Smith's self-contradictions twisting in the air.

But it was not to be simply Al Smith's word against Powell's. The district attorney had gathered a whole team of witnesses to say that Powell had threatened to kill her ex-husband. One after another they took the stand: Anthony Thomas, Leon Farley, Lisa Johnson, Diane Nelson, David Brown. Thomas and Farley, young and uneasy, reluctantly repeated threatening remarks they said they had never taken seriously, but Johnson, Nelson, and Brown told of other more ominous threats and of the day in Diane Nelson's apartment when they heard the loud noise.

Tony Thomas, an eighteen-year-old high school boy who lived with his family in West Village, said Powell once asked him where she could get some acid to throw at her ex-husband, and "a couple of times she said that she was going to kill him." Leon Farley said that Powell asked him laughingly once or twice to beat up Herman after she had seen him in a bar with a blond. Once she spoke to him of wanting to get some acid to throw in Herman's face, but never of guns or killing. The day he helped Powell and his girl friend Lisa Johnson move to Owego, about a week and a half before Herman was shot, he saw Powell's little boy playing next to the truck with a small-caliber bullet.

Farley's sometime girl friend, Lisa Johnson, also known as Lisa Diaz, followed him to the stand, a tiny ashen woman who appeared to be dazed or drugged. She answered in a voice so small and toneless that Judge Dean had to ask Mr. Morehouse, the juror at the far end of the back row who had a little touble with his hearing, if he was picking up the answers. She testified that she had been at Diane Nelson's apartment with Diane and David Brown when Al Smith came in and went to a back room. "I guess something did happen," she whispered. Afterward Powell showed her a book and said "Look. . . . I shot a hole in it." A few days later, when they went to Owego, Lisa not only saw Powell's son playing with a bullet, but she also saw the bullet fall out of the truck, from "under the glove compartment." On the drive back to Ithaca, Lisa testified, when she and Powell and their children were alone in the truck, Powell, who was "very upset and distraught," said that she was going to shoot Herman in the back. Lisa repeated the advice she had given Powell at the time: "Don't shoot him in the back. Shoot him in the front." To her it seemed to be a matter of principle. "It wasn't good to shoot a man in the back," she said.

Diane Nelson sauntered to the witness stand on spike

heels, dressed in a tight yellow pantsuit and a droopy picture hat made of furry polyester fleece. She slouched in the witness chair, hiding under her hat brim, gnashing a large wad of chewing gum, a frightened woman pretending scarcely to notice that she was where she did not want to be—trapped in the midst of great trouble. None of this, she wanted to make clear, was *her* fault. Powell, she said angrily, "is supposed to be a friend and she is putting everybody through this mess."

Before Powell moved to Owego, Diane let her stay in her apartment, sleep in her bedroom, keep things in her dresser drawers. For a while, Diane said, until she stopped listening, Powell told her everything. Powell wanted to throw acid at Herman, to burn his house, to shoot him. She told Diane she had thrown Drano at him, and Diane herself saw the iron—her own iron—sailing out the window of her apartment at Herman Smith. "She dogged him," Diane said. One day, when Diane was at home, Al Smith came to see Powell, and Diane heard a loud noise, which everyone told her was a cap. Powell said she had a gun in her refrigerator, a remark Diane took as a joke—"like, yes, she's keeping it on ice." Still, when others laughed at Powell's threats, Diane took them to heart. She knew that Herman was "messing with white women" and just how angry that made Powell. To Powell she said, "Stay away from him," and to the others, who thought that Powell was kidding, she said, "Yes, she's going to do it. She's crazy."

Powell had a plan. "She was going to figure out some way to get a familylike thing with all three of them. They would go on a trip and she was going to do something to him. . . . I think it was Canada . . . just a familylike thing and get over there and figure out some way she was going to shoot him, think of some reason why she done it and what he was doing. She was going to think of something he was doing to her to cause her to do it." Powell had read about a woman who "killed her old man" and "got sentenced to just one year," so she was going to do the same thing, Diane said, because "she actually thought she was going to get away with it."

Angrily Diane Nelson was telling a story that even the district attorney had not heard before. Joch told Nelson to take out her chewing gum so the jury wouldn't miss a word and asked why she had not said these things to the police or to him or to the judge at the preliminary hearing. "I wanted to stay out of here," she said. "I have been in this place twice for something I had nothing to do with. I just be an innocent bystander who felt sorry for someone and got put in the middle. . . . I was tired of having my name thrown all over the paper. I ain't nobody when you look at it, but I am somebody. . . . I just keep my mouth shut." But even with her mouth shut, Diane Nelson had found herself once again in the middle, with her name thrown all over the paper, and for that she blamed Bernadette Powell.

While Nelson was angry, David Brown was forgetful and crafty. On the stand he didn't remember much except that once or twice Powell said she wanted a gun to kill her husband. Vaguely he recalled being at Diane Nelson's one day when, after Al Smith came in and went to the back of the apartment, "a loud noise went off," which "sounded like either caps or firecrackers or either a gunshot." Diane and Lisa were there too, he said, and another person he referred to as "the other Diane Nelson." If he saw Powell after that, he didn't remember. Brown's testimony didn't amount to much more than Leon Farley's or Tony Thomas's, but added bit by bit to Lisa Johnson's mumbled confidences and Diane Nelson's angry accusations, it was damaging. And Galbraith could not counter the stories. He could only discredit the storytellers.

Under cross-examination Lisa Johnson admitted to "mental troubles." She had literally ripped up her West Village apartment and been sent to the state mental hospital. (She had taken a claw hammer, she said, and "gone around the edges.")

Diane Nelson, a woman supported solely by welfare except when people gave her money, had told one story to the police, another to the D.A., another at the preliminary hearing, and a new one at the trial. And the previous case, in which she had been by her own description "an innocent bystander," involved not only burglary but sodomy and rape, and she herself had been in danger of being charged with a crime. David Brown, already on probation for robbery, had returned from Kentucky at the district attorney's expense to testify against Powell, and within days of his arrival in Ithaca, he was arrested for rape.

When Galbraith rose to cross-examine David Brown, Judge Dean, scrupulous about the touchy business of having on the stand a witness who was himself a criminal defendant, summoned Brown's attorney (the senior partner in Galbraith's firm) and sent the jury out of the courtroom while he listened to the line of questioning Galbraith wanted to pursue. Galbraith wanted the jury to know that Joch had put in a good word for Brown at a bail hearing and then, that very morning, when Brown was arraigned in city court, failed to appear to press the rape charge against him. Apparently free and clear, Brown said he intended to return soon to Kentucky. Joch, he admitted, had bought him a plane ticket. Judge Dean ordered Galbraith not to mention the rape charge in the presence of the jury, but he saw nothing wrong in asking Brown about his travel arrangements with the district attorney. So after the jurors took their seats, Galbraith asked Brown again how he planned to get back to Kentucky. He would go by bus, he said. He planned to pay for the ticket himself.

Galbraith gave up. Against this procession of witnesses attesting, however reluctantly, to Powell's homicidal intent, Galbraith had nothing to offer but their own records of evasion, emotional disturbance, crime, and distortion. When they lied as baldly as David Brown did, he was baffled.

Turning to the night of the shooting, Joch called first a series of witnesses who saw Herman between the time he left his friends' house in Binghamton and the time he arrived at the Ithaca Holiday Inn. The desk clerks at two different Elmira motels had talked to Herman. A taxi dispatcher gave him change for the cigarette machine, and the attendant at the Elmira Arco station gave him gas and directions to another motel. Most of them placed the time roughly at three o'clock in the morning, give or take an hour. None of them observed anything unusual about Smith. None of them thought he was agitated or drunk or carrying a gun. Only one, the night auditor at the Elmira Holiday Inn, created a tangle never to be unsnarled when she testified, emphatically and precisely, that Herman telephoned from the Elmira Holiday Inn and reserved a room at the Ithaca Holiday Inn. But Dorlyn Brown, on duty at the Ithaca Holiday Inn at the time, had already testified that he received no phone call from Herman; and only a few minutes later, according to the Arco attendant, Herman came back to the gas station, looking for another motel.

Georgia Bowman led off another group of witnesses who saw Herman leave the Bowman-Porter apartment with Powell on that last ride. A neat, pudgy white woman edging thirty, she sat stiffly in the witness chair and spoke up. While her boyfriend Horace and Herman had vacation, she said, Herman's son slept at her house with her boy, and each day they all loaded the cars with fishing gear and beer and ham and potato salad and went on a picnic. It was the week of the Fourth of July, and the weather was hot, even for the hills: picnic weather. On Thursday morning, July 6, they were packing to leave for Stewart Park on Cayuga Lake in Ithaca when Powell arrived, accompanied by a young black man, and made a scene, hollering at Herman that she was going to take her son with her. Bowman said she overheard Powell saying to Herman, "If you don't do what I want you to do, I'm going to kill you." Then somehow Powell settled down and they drove away.

On Saturday night, July 8, after they had spent the afternoon fishing and picnicking at GAF Lake, Powell appeared again. At about twelve-thirty, a teenaged boy, a neighbor, came in and told Herman that a woman wanted to see him. Herman left his card game—he'd been playing poker with Horace and Earl Andrews—and spoke with her out on the porch for about ten minutes. Then he came in, awakened and dressed his son, and asked Earl to come along with him. Herman "acted real fidgety," Bowman said, and demanded that Earl "come on right then," but Earl, who was drunk, stayed put. (They had been drinking beer, Bowman said, and "might have drank some gin," and Earl always tended to drink quite a bit more than the others.) All the while Powell stood quietly in the living room, saying nothing. She seemed to Bowman to be "very calm." When she and Herman left the house together, he was wearing blue trousers with a hole in the front and an orange T-shirt bearing the words KAREN FOR SURE. Over one shoulder he carried his son, and over the other the gray trousers in which he was found dead. Bernadette and Herman drove away in separate vehicles, the boy going along in his father's beat-up van. Georgia Bowman watched Herman drive away and never saw him again.

Horace Porter, Bowman's handsome boyfriend, told essentially the same story, adding that although he had known Herman well since 1970 he never knew him to have a drinking problem. He placed Powell's first visit to their house, which Bowman had dated July 6, on July 1, and although he observed that Powell was very angry at the time, he didn't hear her threaten Herman. On that last Saturday night, when Powell stood in his living room in front of the TV set clutching her black purse, she didn't seem to him to be calm. He went over and spoke to her briefly, while she was waiting for Herman to get the boy ready to leave, and although he couldn't remember the conversation, he recalled that she seemed "upset" and "mad."

Another witness who had been in the apartment that evening was Karen Belcher, the Karen of KAREN FOR SURE. She thought it was after one o'clock when Powell arrived, for she remembered going out with Bowman just before one to pick up some food and cigarettes at the convenience store. She remembered that Powell asked Bowman, "Who is 'Karen'?" And she remembered Powell standing in the living room clutching a black pocketbook in front of her "real tight." Herman said, "I'll see you guys later," threw his other pants, the gray ones, over his shoulder, and left.

On short notice Joch called two neighbors to bolster this testimony and almost sank it. Fifteen-year-old Randy Ritter, the boy who went into Bowman's apartment to get Herman, and twenty-two-year-old Vicky Rought, a neighbor who supposedly had been sitting on Bowman's porch, said they overheard Powell threaten to kill Smith; but they disagreed in their elaborate tales on how often Powell appeared that night and when. Ritter placed the time *after* dark, Rought *before*. To reconcile the contradiction, Joch brought on another expert, an astronomy professor from Cornell University, to set for the night in question the scientific limits of twilight—from 8:40 P.M. to 10:53 P.M., a period one might consider, by some stretch of credulity, to be both "before dark" and "after dark" at once. (That still didn't reconcile what Ritter and Rought had to say with the testimony of Georgia Bowman, Horace Porter, and Karen Belcher, all of whom placed Powell's arrival well after midnight; but Joch let that larger contradiction pass—and so did Galbraith.) To Galbraith, Ritter and Rought admitted only that they had talked a good deal with Georgia Bowman and with one another about the incident "and stuff," and that they hadn't talked to the police until "last week."

For the finish, Joch brought back his strongest witness. Senior Investigator Allen G. Smith, the state police firearms examiner, had first taken the stand a few days earlier to describe the ballistics tests he used to determine that both the .22-long rifle bullet that killed Herman Smith and the casing found in Diane Nelson's dresser drawer were fired from the same gun, the revolver on exhibit. He said he had examined Herman's shirt for powder burns and fiber distortion but found nothing of the sort, so he concluded that the fatal shot must have been fired from a distance of "at least a foot and a half." To prove his point he brought along some cotton shirttails into which he had fired from various distances, but Galbraith stopped the demonstration, insisting that the cotton test samples were substantially different from the slick acetate of Herman's shirt.

Now, nearing the end of his case, Joch called Investigator Smith back to the stand with some new exhibits encased in heavy plastic. Investigator Smith had found a shirt with the same fabric content listed on the label of Herman's wild print—65 percent acetate, 35 percent nylon. He had hung pieces of this test shirt from a clothesline and fired at them from various carefully measured distances using .22-long rifle bullets. Then, examining the shirt panels with the naked eye and a binocular microscope, he observed patterns of powder burns, fiber distortion, and "lead wipe." His testimony was long and technical, professional and very exact, and his conclusion, when he slipped it in between Galbraith's loud objections, succinct and firm: "Based on my tests and based on the shirt and the condition in which I received it, the shirt would not have been within thirty-six inches of the muzzle if that weapon were fired at that shirt."

Investigator Smith had already admitted, under cross-examination during his first appearance, that in his search for powder burns he examined only Herman's shirt, not his body or the bedspread, and he didn't see the slippery shirt until after it had been cut, wadded into a plastic evidence bag, and shipped to the lab. And Investigator Weidman had already testified that shortly after the shooting neither Investigator Smith nor "the laboratory" could "testify one way or the other whether or not there was powder burns." But with Investigator Smith's second appearance in court and his definitive testimony, the State firearms laboratory officially changed its mind.

Joch had one last witness, called to attest to Powell's potentially violent nature—Townsend "Bud" Ackerman, head of security at the West Village Apartments. He testified briefly that on May 28, 1978, a Sunday morning, he broke up an altercation between Powell and a man called Jimmy McNeil, who had hurled a bottle that struck her son. She telephoned someone and said, "Brown, bring a gun, because I am going to kill this mother." She used another word, too, Ackerman testified, but for the sake of politeness he would leave it out. "Well, if you please," Joch reminded him, "this is a murder trial," and Ackerman repeated Powell's whole threat: "I'm going to kill this motherfucker." With that, Joch announced that he had concluded the case for the prosecution.

# CHAPTER 6

# DEFENSE

On Wednesday afternoon March 14, when Joch rested his case, Galbraith told Judge Dean that although he would not be fully prepared to present his case until the following morning, he would begin anyway. Then, like a promising horse left at the starting gate, the defense case foundered before it got off the mark. Galbraith called Investigator Edward J. Kelly of the state police to question him about the search of Tom Wallace's apartment, the apartment in which Powell was staying at the time of the shooting. He asked in his most resounding voice, "Okay, Investigator Kelly, on July eleventh, 1978, did you execute a search warrant in connection to this case on premises known as Five Lake Street in Owego, New York?"

And Investigator Kelly answered just as clearly, "No."

Kelly patiently explained that he signed for the return of the warrant after the search, but he didn't sign the warrant itself or take part in the search. He knew nothing about it except that it had been conducted by Investigator Koons, who was not present in court because Galbraith had not called him. Investigator Koons never did come to court, and the business of searching Tom Wallace's apartment was left dangling before the jurors, not only a loose end but a frazzled one. Confounded, Galbraith accepted Judge Dean's offer to adjourn until morning.

When court reconvened, Galbraith set about establishing the story he had outlined in his opening statement: the shooting of Herman Smith was merely the last act in a drama of violence begun years earlier. Sergeant David Eggleston of the Binghamton Police Department brought to court the records of Herman's convictions for burglary in 1969 and assault and possession of an unlicensed firearm in 1970, and his arrest again in 1976 for violating a family-court order of protection and resisting arrest. The district attorney protested furiously this "wholesale slander" of the dead man's character, but Judge Dean ruled that testimony showing Herman's "turbulent nature" was admissible, at least up to a point. He would allow testimony about Herman's arrests only if they led to convictions. Even leaving out all the arrests that came to nothing, it was a suggestive record—a stupid, hotheaded burglary, a wrestling match with a cop, and some drunken potshots fired in the street at an unarmed man.

Others attested to Herman's "turbulent nature." A Binghamton patrolman said Herman ripped his jacket in two when he tried to arrest him for assault. Lieutenant Richard Fundis of the Vestal Police testified that he received two or three cracked ribs struggling to arrest Herman. Powell's younger brother Guydell, who as a teenager lived on and off with Bernadette and Herman, told of being awakened in the middle of the night by the sounds of struggle. Once he found his sister with her hands tied, fighting against Herman, and more than once he called the police. Linda Thompson, a school friend of the Powells, said that one night in the bar at the Binghamton Ramada Inn she saw Herman come in, apparently drunk, pull Bernadette out of her chair and hit her. Sanobia Tarrant, a childhood friend, said that one evening when Bernadette came to console her on the death of her mother, Herman came after his wife, yanked her out of the apartment, kicked her down the stairs, picked her up, and shoved her into a car.

Oscar Lee Powell, age twenty-five, the defendant's brother, continued the litany of abuse. One night at his mother's apartment in Binghamton, sometime between 1971 and 1973, he was awakened by loud noises and ran upstairs to find his sister, her hands tied behind her back, struggling with Herman. Oscar punched Herman, and while the two of them struggled, Bernadette ran from the room and someone called the police. Another time, when he was sitting with his sister in the living room of the house in Vestal, listening to records, Herman burst in and started ripping the place apart. Again he fought hard with Herman until the police came and took Herman away.

Herman was a heavy drinker, Oscar said, and although he appeared at one time to have stopped drinking altogether, in general his drinking had grown progressively heavier since 1974. Although Oscar rarely visited his sister's home, he ran into Herman about once a week, usually at his garage, and always Herman was drinking. Oscar said Herman had a "certain way of acting" when he'd been drinking. He got rowdy and swore a lot, aching for a fight. To Oscar the personality change Herman underwent when he drank seemed so extreme that after his death Oscar described Herman to the police as "an insane guy." Sometimes Herman said he was going to kill Bernadette, but Oscar couldn't specify exactly when he heard that threat, because Herman said it "all the time."

Galbraith called Dorothy Wager, Powell's matrimonial attorney, who came to the stand lugging a bulging pasteboard folder. Slowly, for Mrs. Wager was not be be rushed, Galbraith led her through a dismal recital of legal proceedings during the marriage of Powell and Smith. The list of Herman Smith's offenses against Bernadette Powell was long and grueling, and during the questioning of Dorothy Wager it began to seem interminable, for Wager was painfully slow and careful with her answers. She held on her lap the thick folder of legal papers, filed in no apparent order, and each time she was asked about an incident—an assault, an order of protection, a violation of child support—she thumbed through the papers one by one until she found the particular document to back her up. Some witnesses, like Linda Thompson and Sanobia Tarrant, could report only one brief incident of abuse, while others, like brother Oscar, got some of their dates wrong or their memories mixed, but Dorothy Wager held the whole story in her precariously balanced folder and doggedly rummaged among her random papers until she found precisely what she was looking for. She could not be got around, and she would not be hurried. She drove the district attorney to distraction.

As he cross-examined witnesses, Joch suggested a very different story of the abuse of Bernadette Powell. When Sergeant Eggleston listed Herman's record of arrests for domestic violence, Joch asked him if there was anything in his records to show "whether or not Bernadette Powell was the one that *provoked* the argument in the first place?" Wasn't it fair to say, Joch asked Lieutenant Fundis of the Vestal Police, that the aggression between Powell and Smith "was an equal thing" rather than a case of "one aggressive person?"

"Sometimes, yes," Fundis replied. "Sometimes, no."

Wasn't it true that sometimes she invited him over and then tried to get him arrested on an order of protection? True, said Fundis. And wasn't it true that several times, when Powell's mother called the police, they rushed to Tharp Street only to find no "family affair" in progress? Wasn't it true in fact that "most of the complaints from the mother were totally unfounded?"

"That's correct," said Fundis.

Joch asked Guydell Powell what his sister did just before Herman hit her. Was she arguing with him? Calling him names?

She might be doing anything at all, Guydell said. "She didn't know it was going to come."

Hadn't he ever seen Bernadette physically attack Herman? "No."

Questioning Guydell about the time he came upon his sister struggling with Herman, her hands tied behind her back, Joch made more salacious suggestions. He wanted to know how Bernadette was dressed and whether her feet were tied together.

Guydell said she was wearing "night clothes," and he wasn't sure about her feet.

Joch asked, "Do you know anything about the sex life of your sister with Herman Smith?"

"No," Guydell said, "I didn't really get in— I didn't think that was too much my business."

"That's what I mean," Joch shot back. "You don't know anything about it, right?"

Joch asked Oscar Powell about the time he rushed upstairs at his mother's apartment to find Bernadette pinned down on the bed with her hands tied behind her. Herman had his hand over Bernadette's face, Oscar said, and he was shaking her head from side to side when Oscar burst into the room.

"Did you notice," Joch asked, "whether or not his pants were undone?"

"No," Oscar said.

"Did you notice whether or not his penis was out?"

"No."

"You don't know?"

"No," Oscar said firmly. "I know they weren't."

"How do you know?"

"Because when I got into something with him, this fight, they would have been out then, right?"

"You mean his genitals?"

"Right."

"But when you first came in the room, you don't know whether or not they were out?"

"No."

"Was there anything to indicate whether or not your sister and Herman had already had sex before you came into the room?"

"No."

Later in his cross-examination, Joch brought the matter up again, leading Oscar to say that he had "interfered" in the struggle on his own initiative. "As far as you know," Joch said, "you don't know whether that was a sexual thing or whether that was an actual physical battle, do you?"

"Well, I know it wasn't a sexual thing," Oscar replied.

Joch led Oscar to say that he had heard from his mother of other times when Herman tied up Bernadette. "And you still thought that was not a sexual thing?" Joch asked. Judge Dean sustained Galbraith's objection, and the question, which had been put as argument, remained unanswered. Oscar, Joch suggested, was as bad as his mother, always perversely interfering in Bernadette's marriage. Yes, Oscar said, he interfered—not in every incident he witnessed, but when he felt he had to, and so did his mother. It was a mother's instinct, he said, to protect her child.

Joch also had his own theory of the fight in the Cadillac Lounge. That incident loomed over the trial, foreshadowing the death to come, and Joch brought it up again and again— as if to hold a trial within a trial—first in cross-examining Guydell Powell. Yes, Guydell said, he knew of the bar, and he knew of an incident that occurred there on May 14, 1977, but only because he had been told about it three days later by his sister Tonya. About that account of the incident, being hearsay, he could not be questioned, but Joch asked him nevertheless if, after hearing of the incident, he still believed that his sister Bernadette was afraid of her husband. Yes, Guydell said; from the things he'd seen, he believed she was.

When Oscar took the stand, Galbraith anticipated trouble and brought up the Cadillac Lounge himself. Oscar said he had worked there as a disk jockey from 1975 to 1977. He recalled an evening probably in the summer of 1977 when Bernadette came into his control booth, upset that Herman had "gotten started again." Fifteen minutes later, he said, Herman appeared, asked Bernadette to talk with him in the hallway, and then began raining blows on the top of her head. Oscar again fought with Herman, careening around the bar, until the police arrived. Oscar said he couldn't observe what other people did in the crowded bar during the fight, because he was too busy fighting, but as far as he knew, when the police broke things up Herman had not been stabbed. He had never heard that Herman was taken to the hospital. Cross-examined, Oscar was uncertain whether this incident had happened in 1977 or 1975, and he couldn't remember just why Bernadette had been so upset that night, but his basic story remained unshaken.

Then, with strong suggestions in the air that Bernadette Powell, abetted by her interfering family, was the aggressor in this abusive relationship, Joch undertook the cross-examination of attorney Dorothy Wager. Isn't it routine, he wanted to know, for the family court to issue orders of protection for the merest allegations of intimidation? No, she said, it is not. Isn't it routine for wives to get orders of protection simply for verbal abuse? Not in her experience. Hadn't this Powell-Smith marriage dragged on for an unusually long time? No, Wager said. Weren't there "numerous times" when Powell reconciled with Herman and "numerous times after getting orders of protection when she invited him back into the house?"

Yes, Wager said, "she didn't want to break up the marriage."

And at the hearings on the issue of support, wasn't Powell demanding more money? No, she said, Herman requested the hearings, wanting to pay less. Didn't Powell try to keep the child away from Herman? On the contrary, Powell wanted the child to spend time with his father.

Losing ground, Joch grew personal, suggesting bias and collusion. Why was it that in her law practice two-thirds of her clients were women? Was *she* married? Had *she* ever been divorced? Just how well did she *know* the judge of the family court? Galbraith objected again and again, and Judge Dean interrupted several times to tell Joch to get on with it. But at last Joch's recklessness led Dorothy Wager to a single unguarded phrase. "What was [Powell's] attitude toward the divorce?" he asked.

"The matter speaks for itself," she said. "It was a love-hate relationship. She wanted to keep the marriage going, but she could not live with this man."

"And what evidence and what observations did you make that led you to believe that at times she did in fact hate this man?"

"No," Wager said, backpedaling, "I did not ever form the impression that she hated this man."

"You said it was a love-hate relationship. What did you mean?"

"His attitude seemed to be that way. She was— Her attitude was more love-fear."

"I see," Joch said. "In other words, a moment ago when you said . . . love-hate relationship you were only talking about him, right?"

"Yes," Wager said, "I was."

"Did you misunderstand my question?" Joch asked sarcastically, and Judge Dean, without waiting for Galbraith to object, muttered, "Sustained, sustained, sustained."

Finally Joch asked Wager for her version of the incident at the Cadillac Lounge. Herman "ended up with a stab wound," she said, after "a battle" with Oscar and "others," but witnesses at a family-court hearing on the matter testified that Bernadette "was not actively involved in this."

"Did Herman testify?" Joch asked.

"Herman did."

"Well, who did he say stabbed him in the back?"

"It is my recollection that he was not sure, but he was blaming Bernadette or Oscar."

Dorothy Wager was the eleventh witness to testify for the defense, and until she left the stand almost all of Galbraith's questioning and most of Joch's cross-examination concerned the prolonged abuse of Bernadette Powell at the hands of Herman Smith. As Galbraith told the story, Powell was the unfortunate victim of a hard-drinking, volatile, and brutal husband. As Joch told it, she was a calculating bitch given to kinky sex, greedy manipulation, and violence. Herman's stabbing at the Cadillac Lounge had been replayed again and again—starring Powell as innocent victim in Galbraith's version, or vicious assailant in Joch's—as if it were a kind of dress rehearsal for Herman's shooting, which so far scarcely had been mentioned.

To reopen the important question of powder burns, Galbraith recalled Investigator Eisenberg and read aloud the testimony he gave at the preliminary hearing about an "irregularity," possibly a powder burn, around the wound in Herman Smith's chest. Eisenberg remembered what he had said at that hearing: that the reddening might be a powder burn or perhaps blood, difficult as it was to tell on dark skin. But now he was quite sure he had seen nothing more than blood—"blood in the hole and blood on the chest." That was that on the subject of powder burns and firing distance, for Galbraith had no firearms experts of his own to call.

Then, to talk at last about the night of July 8, 1978, the night Herman Smith died, Galbraith called Michael Thomas to the stand. A stocky seventeen-year-old Ithaca High School student who lived in the West Village Apartments, he was the younger brother of prosecution witness Tony Thomas and, he said, "good friends" with Powell. When she lived in West Village, he stopped by her apartment almost every day to talk and play a game of rummy. He was the "black man in his twenties," as Georgia Bowman described him, who accompanied Powell when she went to the Bowman-Porter apartment to "hassle" Herman shortly before his death. Bowman placed that visit on Thursday July 6. Thomas was sure it took place on his day off from work, Saturday July 8. But his story differed most from Bowman's in his description of Powell's behavior.

As he told it, Powell did not raise her voice or argue or threaten. They were driving to Binghamton to visit Powell's brother Guydell in the hospital and stopped off at Herman's in Endicott just "to check on her son." Finding no one at home, they waited, and within five minutes Herman came to pick up his picnic cooler. At his suggestion, they followed him back to the Bowman-Porter apartment to see the boy, and Powell questioned Herman about the child's appearance. "Look at him, Herman. Look at his hair. When was the last time you combed it? Look at his feet. When is the last time he took a bath?" It was not an argument, Thomas said. She was just complaining "like any mother would."

Cross-examining, Joch asked Thomas if Powell and Herman hadn't quarreled publicly at a Little League baseball game in Ithaca. No, he said, there was no trouble of any kind. As to the rest of the talk around West Village, Thomas never heard Powell threaten Herman or mention acid or guns. And no one ever told him about a gun going off at Diane Nelson's apartment.

Joch wanted to know if Powell ever tried to keep her son away from his father. No, Thomas said, but she did say once that "she really didn't like [her son] staying with him because he used to mess with little white girls, younger, thirteen year old, around that age, and she thought that it would make a bad influence. . . ." She was not jealous but concerned. And on that Saturday afternoon at Georgia Bowman's she was doubly concerned because Herman was drunk. As he drove off in his van he was weaving a little, and Powell said to Thomas, "Look at him. He's drunk already. It's not even two o'clock yet. I hope he doesn't get in an accident with [my son] in the truck."

So, Joch crowed, you thought "he was drunk because she told you that."

No, Thomas said, he *knew* Herman was drunk. He could see for himself—Herman's red eyes, his slurred speech, his unsteady movements negotiated cautiously and "real slow."

Each time Joch implied that Powell was at fault, Thomas offered more unsavory information about Herman. Joch tried to intimidate him with big words, but Thomas said simply, "Speak English." He was a big, straightforward, likable kid who admired his friend Bernadette, and no construction the district attorney might put on things could keep him from telling his story his way. Seeing that, Joch stopped asking questions.

That left only one witness to finish the case for the defense, and after a short recess, Galbraith called Bernadette Alyce Powell. She stepped to the stand, wearing like a uniform her familiar layered jerseys, with the big silver cross squarely in the middle of her chest. She crossed her legs demurely at the ankle and grasped one hand firmly in the other, as though only by binding herself down could she keep herself from flying apart. She fastened her eyes on Galbraith, as he had told her to do, and began in a deep, quiet voice to answer his questions. Her answers were clipped and precise, like prerecorded messages.

Galbraith eased her into the examination. She was twenty-six years old, she said, and lived with her son in Binghamton, where she went to school by day at Broome County Tech and worked at night as a nurse's assistant at a nursing home. She had graduated from high school in Binghamton and studied computer science for two years at Rochester Business Institute, and then for three or four years she worked at GAF, a film-processing plant. On April 18, 1970, when she was just eighteen, she said, she married Herman Smith, a man from Mississippi she had known "over a year."* Their son—her only child—was born February 18, 1972.

Herman drank, she said, mostly on weekends. He bought "those little tiny liquor bottles I guess you can fit in your back pocket" and drank them down. And when he did that, his behavior changed. He became "uncontrollable." Sometimes when he drank, he abused her. Powell described those incidents in a terse shorthand, as though such abuse were so common that at the merest allusion everyone would know fully what had happened. "Put me in the bathtub, turn on

*Powell and Galbraith got the date wrong. Actually, she married April 13, 1971. April 1970, two months before the birth of her first child, was approximately when she and Herman *wanted* to marry.

the hot water, extreme hot water, then cold. When I was sleeping, tie me up where I'd be helpless. I couldn't wake up out of sleep fast enough. Crush ashes into my sides when I'd be sleeping. There were so many incidents." When Herman was drinking, she felt scared, she said. "I was young, so I was scared." He hit her with rings on his hands, he kicked her, he tied her up. But there were too many incidents to remember, and even when Galbraith questioned her about a particular incident, she recalled only bits and pieces, shards of broken memory, none of them adding up to anything like an event. Galbraith asked about one time Herman tied her up, the time Guydell ran up the street to call the police. "I was sleeping . . ." she said. "I was weak and he had just started— He got some kind of belt or something. I don't know what type of thing it was. And just tied my hands up. I was weak, I vaguely remember, in the situation. But I remember the pain I was going through. How it came about I really can't remember that. But I do remember, you know, just tying my hands up. And he always did this while I was sleeping."

Vaguely she remembered being kicked down the stairs, dragged from her car, beaten up; and she remembered sitting in her living room while Herman slashed and smashed the furniture and feeling "real cold." Galbraith questioned her about the time Herman attacked her in the parking lot at the Philadelphia Sales discount store, but she said, "I cannot remember the incident." There were other incidents of abuse that she did not remember at all, she said, until she heard witnesses testify to them in court.

Usually, she said, Herman beat her up so often—about twice a week—that she devised a "code" with her mother, who automatically called the police if Bernadette didn't answer the phone. She was afraid to have Herman arrested, though, because he swore he would kill her if she did. She was hospitalized more than once, and although she got orders of protection, he violated them and beat her up again. She believed he might beat her to death. Finally, she said,

"I wanted to just get away from him. I was older. You know, when I was young, I was under the belief you accepted your man for better or worse. Well, I'm older now and I couldn't take any more beatings. And [my son] was getting older too. And I did not want him to see all that." She got a divorce.

But instead of ending her bad times, divorce made them worse. She wrote some bad checks, mistakenly believing that Herman's support payments, made directly to the bank, were on time. She had to post a bond and make restitution. She had to sell her house, and knowing nothing of banks, she foolishly took the money in cash and then lost it. She moved to subsidized housing in Ithaca and went on welfare. At that time, she said, when things were just about as bad as they could be, she made the acquaintance of Diane Nelson and Lisa Johnson and David Brown. She even moved in with Diane Nelson, temporarily, for "less than a week," before she moved to Owego to start anew. But in all the time she lived in Ithaca, she never did meet a man named Al Smith.

On the day she went with Michael Thomas to Endicott to check on her son (like Thomas, she said it was Saturday July 8), she had no quarrel with Herman. That evening, after doing some cooking and reading and listening to reggae music, she left Tom Wallace's apartment in Owego about ten o'clock and drove in about forty minutes' time to the Bowman-Porter apartment in Binghamton. She didn't see Randy Ritter or anyone else on the porch, she said. And she didn't have a talk on the porch with Herman. She simply knocked on the door and waited in the living room while Herman got their son ready to leave. Herman told another man, Earl Andrews, that he would drive him home, but Earl seemed to be drunk. So Herman took their son in his van, saying he had her child's bike and clothes in Endicott, and Powell followed in her truck. Still, she said, there was no argument.

She told the rest quickly, repeating what she had said in her statement to the police and so many times afterward. She described her efforts to get help after the gun "went off" and her cooperation with the police investigators, and then Galbraith asked her his most important questions.

"Did you ever buy a pistol from Al Smith?"

"No, sir, I did not."

"Have you ever owned a pistol?"

"No, sir, I have not."

"Bernadette, when the gun went off at the Holiday Inn, did you mean to kill Herman Smith?"

"No, sir, I did not."

It was a strong finish, but Joch, waiting to cross-examine, had planned a strong opening. "Would you examine that, please?" he asked, handing her the gun, people's exhibit 44.

"I'll look at it," she said, "but I'm not going to touch it."

Except for the moment when she shot her ex-husband, she said, she had never held that gun or any other gun in her hand. She had heard Investigator Eisenberg testify that she held his gun and reenacted the shooting at the police barracks, but she was sure that "never happened."

"You're saying that Al Smith came here and testified that he sold you a gun and that that is not true; is that correct?" Joch asked.

"Yes."

"Do you know Al Smith?"

"No, sir, I do not."

With brittle politeness she answered all his questions about the witnesses against her. She didn't know, sir, whether they knew Herman. She didn't know, sir, what motive they might have for lying about her.

"You don't have to call me sir," Joch snapped.

"I know I don't, sir," she said.

How about the Cadillac Lounge incident, Joch wanted to know. Wasn't it true that Oscar called her down to the bar because Herman was there with a white woman she knew, Patricia Williams? Wasn't it true that Oscar dragged Herman into the men's room? And wasn't it true that there in the men's room Bernadette stabbed him in the back? And wasn't it true that later Bernadette attacked Patricia Williams? No, sir. No, sir. No, sir, came the answers. She remembered the fight between Herman and Oscar and, from the family-court hearing, she remembered that Herman *accused* her of stabbing him. But she didn't do it, didn't even know until the hearing that Herman had been stabbed. And as for Patricia Williams, she knew no one by that name.

Joch returned to the question of Herman Smith's drinking pattern. He drank at home on the weekends, she said, but during the week, when he was away from home during the day, he came home drunk just about every other day. Then he would force her into the scalding shower and hold her there, crying, until her body burned and blistered. Then he would dry her off and apologize.

"All right," Joch said, "in those days were you having sex regularly with him?"

"No, sir."

"Well, were you having it at all?"

"Yes, sir."

"And about how often were you having it at that time?"

"After he beat me up."

"After he beat you up?"

"Sometimes, yes, sir. They were never normal."

"So the sex was always related to some of this physical abuse?"

"Sometimes, sir, yes. It was only natural when we first got married."

"It was without physical abuse at first?"

"Yes, sir."

"And then two years later it started to be connected to the physical abuse?"

"I would say so, yes."

About the increasing abuse and the increasingly erratic sex life she had said nothing to anyone, afraid that Herman would "do worse."

Didn't the house belong to Herman too, Joch demanded. And didn't Bernadette and her mother call the police at the "drop of a pin"? Wasn't it a fact that she "often called the police when there was no need to? . . . and that the police came to [the] house on numerous occasions where there was absolutely nothing wrong except that the phone was off the hook?"

Well, she thought that had happened only once or twice, but it was difficult to remember. There were so many incidents. "I remember going to the hospital," she said, but "I can't remember what the incident was about. . . . The incidents I have sat here and heard I would never have thought of them." She marveled that the witnesses could remember. Joch was still taking her back through "incidents" when Judge Dean adjourned court for the day, and she was still trying to remember.

The next morning Powell took the stand again, and Joch again set out to portray her as the conniving woman, scheming to do in poor Herman Smith. Why did she refer to the furniture Herman paid for and later smashed up as "hers"? Because, she said, she cleaned it and took care of it. That was her job. Why had she told the Endicott Police, falsely, that Herman was giving out drugs to young kids? Because she was concerned about her son's welfare. Wasn't she jealous of Herman? No. Hadn't she told Investigator Eisenberg she was jealous of Herman? No. Didn't she ask Patricia Davis to lie for her and say that Herman was using drugs? No, she said. Who is Patricia Davis?

Joch came back to her sex life: "Do you know what a masochist is?" he asked.

"Yes, I do."

"Have you ever heard of people who like to be hurt? Are you a person who likes to be hurt?"

"No, sir, I am not."

Joch tried to pin down the dates of one incident after another, although Powell said repeatedly that she could not remember dates and had to rely upon her attorney to supply them for her. She grew increasingly confused. Finally, bewildered by Joch's chronology, she said sharply, "I think you represent the people well. You have my mind in a fog."

Galbraith, seeing her stumble again toward hysteria, shouted at her, "Be quiet!"

She liked her house and her life in Vestal, she said, and if only Herman had been different she would have stayed there forever. But because they needed the money, she had to go to work, and Herman accused her of seeing other men at work. He wanted her to stay home and keep house and keep herself for him. In that sense, she agreed with Joch, she "provoked" Herman's assaults on her. "Maybe if I had stayed home like he wanted me to stay home, maybe that would have made a difference. In other words, he wanted me to stay in that house, nowhere else, sir. If I had to stay home, certainly things would never have happened."

Joch still had cards to play for the prosecution—exhibits 84 and 85, application forms for recertification for public assistance filled out and signed in the name of Bernadette Powell. Joch handed her people's exhibit 85, an application dated March 1978. She identified her printing on page one, but she didn't recognize the handwriting on page two. She denied receiving benefits in March, April, May, and June of 1978, while she was working at IBM. "If they came to the house I did not receive them," she said, but several young girls had lived with her at West Village, serving as baby-sitters. "If there is any welfare fraud I would know who the culprits are."

Joch handed her people's exhibit 84, an application dated May 10, 1978, and again she recognized only bits of it. "This part up here is my printing," she said, "but down here is not my writing."

"Now," Joch asked, "didn't you tell social services and fill out this application and sign your name to it on May ninth or May tenth, 1978 indicating that [your niece] still lived with you?"

"No, sir," she said firmly.

"Do you see the part that says 'the following people are in my family, live with me, and need—continue to need public assistance'?" he asked, pointing to the document she held in her hand.

"Yes, sir."

"And isn't [her] name . . . listed?"

"Yes, sir."

"You signed your name to that?"

"It appears to be my signature," she said, "but I did not sign anything to that effect. . . ."

"Even though that appears to be your signature you didn't sign it?"

"No, sir, I did not. . . ."

From that point on, Powell denied almost everything Joch brought up. She didn't know Leon Farley at all. She never had bullets in her truck or anywhere else. She never had a gun or fired a gun at Diane Nelson's or anyplace else. As for the empty casing in the dresser at Nelson's apartment, well you were "liable to find anything in Diane's dresser drawers." She never telephoned anyone to bring her a gun, as Ackerman the security man testified, and she certainly never said she was going to "kill the motherfucker." She never saw Randy Ritter or Vicky Rought or any other people on the porch at Georgia Bowman's. She never mentioned a blonde or a Canadian vacation to Diane Nelson or spoke to Michael Thomas about Herman and little white girls. On the night of July 8, Herman was not wearing a T-shirt saying KAREN FOR SURE; he left the Bowman-Porter apartment wearing the clothes in which he died. She never threatened Herman in any way. She never told Diane Nelson or Lisa Johnson or David Brown or Leon Farley or Michael Thomas or Tony Thomas or anyone else that she wanted acid or a gun or the death of Herman Smith.

Joch wanted to know whether, on the night Herman died, she felt her life in jeopardy. Yes, she said, "both of ours, my son and mine." She didn't think Herman would deliberately harm the child, but she feared that "anything coulda went wrong and maybe got shot by accident." So she didn't try to bargain with Herman, and she never thought of leaving her son in the truck and trying to make her own escape. Each time Herman left the truck he warned her not to try anything, and she didn't. Each time he left the truck, she sat there, sometimes for "over five minutes," sometimes "maybe less"—she didn't know—patting her son's back, "watching the door, waiting for him to come back out, just sitting there, tears coming down my eyes. That's all. Quiet."

The only thing Powell was uncertain about was that moment on the bed at the Holiday Inn when the gun went off. Joch badgered her, trying to pin her down.

"What was the farthest distance away from his chest that this gun was when you say the gun fired?"

"I don't know, sir. We were real close, though. I did not leave the bed."

"Do you have an estimate of the farthest distance away it could have been?"

"No, sir, I do not."

"In other words, it could have been ten feet away?"

"No, sir."

"Had to be closer than ten feet?"

"Yes, I was on the bed, so whatever you estimate."

"Could it have been more than two feet away?"

"I don't know, sir."

"Could it have been more than one foot away?"

"I don't know, sir."

"Are you telling us that the gun could have been touching his chest when it went off, as far as you recall?"

"I don't know, sir."

She did know that the phrase in her police statement—"a hand's distance" away—was not her own. The wording, she said, was Investigator Eisenberg's. "He offered that," she said. "I was cooperative. Whatever he wanted to put in there I let him put in there." She hadn't "studied" Herman's position at the time the gun went off, she said, so she didn't remember exactly how he was facing or where the gun was pointing or what position her hand was in at the time. He jumped and rose up off the bed just before the gun went off, but she couldn't remember how much of his upper torso had raised up or what angle it took in relation to the bed. She was positive only that she never told the police she pulled the trigger *intentionally*. And the police were wrong about one other thing—that business about her taking the truck keys out of her purse. The keys were on the dresser in the motel room, she said, and that incident, as the police described it, positively never happened.

Powell had been on the stand for three hours, sitting straightbacked, repeating steadily, "No, sir; No, sir; No, sir," when Judge Dean adjourned the court for lunch. She resumed the stand just before two o'clock, and Galbraith and Joch skirmished back and forth, back and forth, about the welfare forms, a hard blow to Powell's credibility. Ten minutes later it was over, and both the defense and the prosecution rested their cases. Court adjourned until nine o'clock the next morning when the attorneys would make their final summations to the jury.

# CHAPTER 7

# VERDICT

In summation, it is the unfortunate position of the defense attorney to have to go first, leaving the last word to the prosecutor. Galbraith studied his notes, got a shoeshine and a haircut, and put on his best dark suit. He had about an hour to convince the jury that Bernadette Powell should be acquitted.

Everyone agreed, he said, that at about 7:40 A.M. on July 9, 1978, "Bernadette Powell had in her hand a pistol" which discharged, killing Herman Smith. But "an important question," to which he turned at once, was whether Powell purchased that gun and the bullet that killed Herman. He found "several very good reasons" to doubt that she did. Al Smith was "a suspected gun dealer," he said, "and when such a person believes himself to be in trouble it is very easy to say what he thinks the police want to hear." And Al Smith, trying to get his story straight, made what Galbraith called "one critical error." First he told the police he sold Powell a box of short bullets, but the police discovered Herman had been shot with a long bullet, and Al Smith had to amend his statement to include five rounds of long ammunition. Then the ballistics experts discovered Herman had been killed with a long *rifle* cartridge, a third type of bullet, different from the others, which Al Smith hadn't mentioned at all. And what happened to all that ammunition? The police searched everywhere and never found it, and there were no other bullets in the gun. "Can you imagine . . . a person cold-bloodedly plotting to murder another person," Galbraith asked, "and then as a weapon using a small-caliber pistol with one bullet in it?" In any event, Powell knew nothing about guns, while Herman certainly did. Since Herman once owned an R.G. Industries .22-caliber revolver, it stood to reason that he might have gone back to his source for another one.

The witnesses who backed up Al Smith, Galbraith said, testified only about a loud noise in the back room. None claimed to have seen the gun. He "could spend a lot of time talking about the inconsistencies" in the statements of those witnesses, Galbraith claimed, but instead he attacked their characters. "You saw these people on the witness stand," he said. "You heard the way they testified. I think you know something by now about the kinds of people they are. . . . I don't believe that you ladies and gentlemen of the jury could convict this woman of murder on the basis of testimony like that and still sleep at night. You . . . have seen a seller of illegal firearms, a convicted robber, a woman who was recently in a mental institution, and another woman who probably belongs in one. They are a tight little group . . . with less-than-average intelligence who live together on the edge of the criminal world." As for young Randy Ritter and Vicky Rought, Galbraith dismissed their testimony as the product of overactive young imaginations. The jury must be careful, he said, to compare the suspect testimony of the prosecution witnesses with "the credible objective evidence . . . in this case, the stuff that there can't be any doubt about," such as the medical evidence that "at the time in the evening when these events all started Herman was legally intoxicated."

Briefly Galbraith summarized Powell's account of the night's ride, arguing that all the circumstantial evidence—right down to the partially empty orange-soda can and the ashtrays filled with cigarette butts at the Holiday Inn—"entirely corroborates" everything Powell said. Then he came to the critical moment of the shooting. "Now we'd all like to know I think how far away the gun was from Herman when it went off," he said, but "the physical evidence in this case doesn't give us the answer to that question," He reminded the jury of Investigator Weidman's testimony that gunpowder residue probably would have fallen off the shirt, and he argued that no one could be sure that the hole in the shirt actually *was* a bullet hole. The shot might have gone directly into Herman's chest, producing on his skin the stippled effect Investigator Allen G. Smith said he would expect to see, the reddening Investigator Eisenberg said at the preliminary hearing he *had* seen. The "only fair conclusion" from all that muddled testimony, Galbraith said, is "that there is no way of knowing from the ballistics test and the circumstantial evidence here whether that pistol was six feet or six inches away from Herman Smith when it went off." Since "we simply don't have the facts," he said, even Investigator Allen G. Smith, the firearms expert, "was not permitted to testify as to any conclusion." (But despite Galbraith's objections at the time, Investigator Smith *had* offered a conclusion—that "the shirt would not have been within thirty-six inches of the muzzle"—and the jury had heard it.)

Joch might imply "that Bernadette Powell stood coolly across the room from her ex-husband as he slept and aimed the pistol at his heart and pulled the trigger." But considering "the angle of the bullet and the position of the body," Galbraith argued, if Powell had "been standing any distance away from Herman Smith when that firearm discharged [she] would have had to have been standing on the ceiling. . . . Ladies and gentlemen," he asked, "couldn't this have happened in exactly the way that Bernadette Powell described to you?"

But that question suggested another: "Is she a believable person?" Certainly the district attorney "interjected a lot of innuendos" about Powell's "supposed vicious criminal his-

tory," Galbraith said, yet after a court hearing on the notorious Cadillac Lounge incident, Powell was never charged
with a crime while Herman Smith was sentenced to thirty
days in jail. Powell was no criminal, but a woman afraid.
And given Herman's record, she had good reason to fear
him. As for the business with the social services department,
Galbraith added, "I am not sure exactly what that was,"
but the surest way to prove fraudulent receipt of welfare
payments is to produce the canceled checks, endorsed by
the recipient, and that the prosecutor did not do.

For the jurors, he said, "the essential question in this case
is really what was going on in Bernadette Powell's mind
when that gun went off. That's really what this case is all
about." Certainly the pistol was in her hand. And surely her
finger must have been on the trigger. But "ladies and gentlemen," he said, "unless you find beyond any reasonable doubt
that Bernadette Powell not only intended to fire that pistol
but she intended to kill her ex-husband when she did it, and
that she was not doing this while in a state of extreme
emotional disturbance as it is called, then I tell you and I
believe Judge Dean will instruct you that you may not find
this woman guilty of murder."

Galbraith might have stopped there, ending with a little
flourish, but instead he went on, defensively plucking at
loose ends. Even if Powell *did* threaten Herman, if she *did*
say she wanted to "kill some motherfucker," such remarks
are merely the "kind of language that you hear all the time
from black people when they are talking." And if she *did*
shoot him intentionally, why didn't she just drive away?
Galbraith was scraping bottom, repeating himself, dragging
up defensive arguments, contradicting his client.

Then, running down, he told the jury that Powell was
afraid of something far worse than physical violence. She
was afraid "that her ex-husband was going to steal her son
away from her." "How would any mother react in the face
of that kind of threat?" he asked rhetorically, bringing an

obvious answer to mind. Until that moment no one had advanced such a strong motive for Bernadette Powell to murder Herman Smith.

"When you put what she said together with all the concrete objective evidence that you have in this case, it simply doesn't add up to murder," he concluded and sat down, hitching up his trousers so as not to spoil the crease. But what *did* it add up to? Manslaughter, perhaps, if Galbraith had argued that Powell shot Herman Smith in self-defense or in a state of extreme emotional disturbance; but he did not. Instead he argued that the shooting was "probably really more accidental than self-defense." He granted the first part of the D.A.'s case—that Powell had shot Herman Smith. And the second part—that she bought the gun and planned murder—he skimmed over, having no evidence to dispute it but Powell's own story, the story he didn't like to tell. He told it briefly, unconvincingly, offering no affirmative defense, and got caught up instead in the prosecution's version, for he knew *that* was a story a jury would believe.

So many of the prosecution witnesses, like David Brown and Lisa Johnson and Diane Nelson, seemed to be marginal figures, living on the verge of vagrancy, that when he first took the case, Galbraith hoped they might just drift away and vanish before the trial. When he heard that David Brown had left town, he laughed at the prospect of the D.A.'s case slipping away, witness by witness, over the county line. So promising was the fantasy that he mistook it for a strategy: to win the case he need only postpone. But the trial came and so did the prosecution witnesses to tell their damning stories, and Galbraith still had no story of his own, no firearms expert to corroborate Powell's account of the shooting, no psychiatric experts to explain the connection between Powell's history as a battered woman—the only "case" he had—and the events of July 8–9, 1978, to explain "what was going on in Bernadette Powell's mind when that gun went off," which he himself said was "really what this case is all about."

Joe Joch, on the other hand, had a story. And when he stood up in his scuffed shoes to summarize it, he was the very model of a good, hardworking public servant, unconcerned with tailoring, caring only for justice. His limp misshapen flannel trousers, permanently bent, made him appear to be forever crouched, earnestly ready. And indeed he was.

He set out first to rehabilitate his witnesses. Galbraith had claimed they were all alike, but in fact, Joch said, they were alike in only one way. They were reluctant to testify. It was not to their advantage to testify, he insisted, but they told the truth, and "the truth was that they knew very, very well that she hated this man—this love-hate relationship that Mrs. Wager testified to and then tried to back out of right away." It was that love-hate relationship, "the intensity of feeling that remained between these two people" that was "the motive in this case."

Whether Herman was a problem drinker was not an issue, Joch said. Drinking was not a crime. But what seemed curious to Joch was that Herman left Horace Porter's with Powell that night, rather than cause trouble there, and that he "begged" Earl Andrews to come with him. It is hard to understand, Joch said, "how a person who has the courage to go and get in a fight with a man is going to be a shrinking violet when it comes to a woman." But "just because a man is big and strong and brave with other men doesn't mean that he is necessarily not going to be manipulated by a woman."

Now that the jury had some facts, he said, it took nerve for Powell to stick to a story that left so many questions unanswered. For instance, how could Powell have grabbed the gun as she said? Any man stuffing a stubby revolver into his pants would shove it far down and anyone who wanted to draw it out would have to do so very deliberately and then shift it to grip the trigger. And how far away was the gun when it went off? Investigator Allen G. Smith's tests proved to Joch that no matter how slippery the fabric or how carelessly the shirt was handled, if the gun were fired close to it, some particles of residue would remain embedded in the cloth. And the downward trajectory of the bullet, Joch said (although there had been no testimony on this point), was "consistent with getting up from the bed, walking over, getting this gun from wherever she had it concealed, walking over to the left shoulder, standing over his left shoulder, pointing the gun down, and firing." For someone trying to murder someone and get away with it, Joch said, this was not a bad scenario.

Afterward Powell stayed around and talked to the police because "she is very, very smart and she is very, very calculating and very cold-blooded." In court she made "a very good witness, very cool, had everything down pat." But it was up to the jurors to be "tough minded" with Powell. They had sworn during *voir dire* that they didn't "believe for a minute that a man is more capable of evil intent than a woman." Now they had to judge her as they would a man.

As for Powell's history of abuse at the hands of Herman Smith, Joch said it couldn't have been as terrible as she claimed. Usually Herman used no weapons, and he injured her seriously enough for her to be hospitalized only once. To hear Joch tell it, it didn't sound so bad. But the worst that could happen to a couple going through such "domestic difficulties" happened to them, he said: they got involved with "a hotshot lawyer" (Dorothy Wager) who would "exaggerate the difficulties" between them and "use their child as a pawn." Despite this conflict, Joch argued, there was no reason to think that Herman was unusually angry on the last night of his life. No, it was Powell who was angry and aggressive. She didn't go to pick up her son. She went to get Herman. She abused him and threatened him. And then she killed him.

The prosecution, Joch said, offered hard evidence that the gun could not have been fired as Powell claimed. And what did the defense counter with? A few instances of abuse. On one hand, the prosecution offered proof beyond a reasonable doubt, while on the other hand the defense offered "Bernadette Powell taking the stand and saying that everybody is wrong except me. Bernadette Powell coming here and saying, 'I don't know, sir. I don't remember, sir. It didn't happen, sir. I never met him, sir. I never had a gun, sir.' " For Powell's story, Joch said, there was no basis but her own assertion, and against that he had set a story of his own about a scheming and vindictive woman, a vicious, cold-blooded killer.

Nothing remained but for Judge Dean to charge the jury on the law they must apply to their deliberations and to lay out the options they had on the verdict. He set his hand to it three or four times, stirring the odd bits of legalistic jargon into a lumpy sludge. The jurors listened with puzzled care and, soon after they retired to deliberate, sent out a request for a written summary of the possible verdicts. He gave them five choices: If they thought Powell intentionally killed Herman Smith, they could find her guilty of murder in the second degree. If they thought she killed him intentionally but only under the influence of an "extreme emotional disturbance," they could find her guilty of manslaughter in the first degree. If they found that she had not intended to kill Herman Smith but that he died as a result of her reckless conduct, they could find her guilty of manslaughter in the second degree. And if they found that Herman Smith's death resulted not from her reckless disregard of risks she could foresee, but from her failure to recognize dangers at hand, then they could find her guilty of criminally negligent homicide. Mentioned last, as an afterthought, was the possibility they might think the state had failed to prove that Bernadette Powell caused, intentionally or not, the death of Herman Smith. In that case, the jury could find her not guilty.

At Galbraith's request, Dean very briefly instructed the jury on one other option—the "defense of justification." The penal law entitled a person to use physical force upon another person, he said, "when and to the extent he reasonably believes it is necessary to defend himself from what he reasonably believes to be the use by the other person of unlawful physical force, or the imminent use of unlawful physical force against him." He (the law always said "he") was not entitled to use "deadly force" unless threatened by deadly force, and he could not claim self-defense if he had provoked the conflict in the first place. Powell was claiming this defense of justification, Judge Dean said, and the State had the burden of disproving it. But Dean, like Galbraith, failed to explain to the jury how it might be applied to this case.

At 2:55 P.M. the jurors retired to the jury room to begin deliberations. Within minutes, foreman Caesar George took a straw poll and came up with twelve votes for guilty of second-degree murder, but to the consternation of a few of the jurors who wanted to be done with it, he insisted they go over all the evidence together before recording a final verdict. At 3:45 they returned to the courtroom to hear the clerk read out, at their request, the testimony of Investigator Eisenberg, Dr. Posso, motel clerk Dorlyn Brown, firearms expert Investigator Allen G. Smith, and gun salesman Al Smith. At 5:55 they went back to the jury room, and ten minutes later they went out to dinner.

They returned to the jury room at 8:20, and twenty minutes later they came back to the courtroom asking for the revolver and the test panels of shirt fabric prepared by Investigator Allen G. Smith. At 8:45 they went back to the jury room, but within half an hour they returned to court with a written request to visit room 253 at the Holiday Inn. They wanted "to look at the bed, heights, distances between the beds, walls, and chairs." Judge Dean denied the request because the law allows such trips to the scene of the crime only before summations are presented, but he granted their other request—that they be given the shirt Herman was wearing when he died. Half an hour later, at 10:00, they adjourned to the Ramada Inn, a few blocks away, for the night.

The next morning, at 9:15, they took up deliberations again, and at 10:00 they sent out a message announcing they had reached a verdict. Altogether they had spent a little under two and a half hours on their deliberations, and in that time none of them underwent a change of heart.

"One thing about this jury," the foreman said after it was all over, "is that they really stuck to the evidence pertaining to what happened that night—not to any battering she received. They really were convinced that she had planned it, and they didn't let the reason why she planned it get involved in their thinking."

"All the stuff about battering," one juror said, "was neither here nor there really, as far as we were concerned."

Said another, "It all boiled down to what happened that night."

And what did happen that night? What story did the jurors construct from the fragmentary accounts they had heard? Most of them believed that the gun that killed Herman Smith arrived at the Holiday Inn in the pocketbook of Bernadette Powell. But it was not Al Smith, the gun salesman, who convinced them. One juror said that Al Smith giving testimony looked as though he were sitting on a hot stove, yet his status as a mailman, a government employee, lent him credibility. Another juror, unimpressed, said, "Well, I guess they hire all kinds down there now." And it was difficult for these upstanding, white, long-time Ithacans to accept the accounts of the "low life" people who paraded to the witness stand one after another to back up Al Smith's story. They seemed to be hoodlums, drug addicts, welfare recipients, "coloreds" who lived "over there" in public housing, indiscriminately producing dependent children. Who could take their word for anything? The jurors were confused by conflicting accounts, unable accurately to evaluate the character and the word of people apparently so different from themselves. When foreman George advised them to pay little attention to the testimony of "transients" in the community, many of the jurors had already made up their minds to do just that. They decided it was best, as one of them put it, not to take "nobody's word for anything," so they dismissed the "shady testimony" of most of the "transients" and "friends" who testified against Powell. But they identified Powell, despite her demure appearance and her exaggerated silver cross, with those "friends." She, like them, was black. That she was "supposed to be an educated person" only made worse her "carousing around" with the kind of people who testified for the prosecution. If the witnesses against her were suspect, so was she.

She was doubly suspect because she claimed to be a battered woman. Some jurors thought she asked for abuse or enjoyed it, as Joch suggested. Others thought she made up or exaggerated the incidents, as Joch also suggested. Many, following Joch's lead, paradoxically entertained both views at once. As one juror said, with remarkable logic, "We all wondered why, if it was as bad as she said it was, she didn't just leave a whole lot sooner. Personally I think she asked for a lot of it. But even if she didn't deserve it, she didn't have to make such a big thing out of it."

They'd caught her out in other lies, too, like the lie about the welfare fraud. One young white male juror, harboring other resentments, said, "She used being black and being a woman as an unfair advantage to get herself an exceptional job at IBM, and then she had the nerve to apply for more welfare." And they'd watched her, seeming so calm, so detached, yet with anger in her eyes, anger in the way she snapped back at the district attorney, who was, after all, only doing his job for the people. (After the trial there was some stink about the D.A. beating up his wife, but none of them could see what his personal problems had to do with anything.) In the eyes of most of the jurors, Bernadette Powell was, as one of them put it, "a real cold bitch."

So they discounted the testimony of both Powell and her adversaries, and they went instead "entirely on the facts." The facts were physical. The facts had to do with angles of entry and powder burns and particles and fabric weave. The facts were exclusively in the possession of a single witness— Senior Investigator Allen G. Smith of the New York State

Police, firearms expert. Hadn't he cut test panels of the same fabric that made up the shirt of Herman Smith? Hadn't he hung them on a clothesline and fired at them, using .22-long rifle bullets, from various precisely measured test distances? Twelve inches, eighteen inches, twenty-four inches, thirty-six inches. Hadn't he examined the test panels for patterns of powder burns and fiber distortion and "lead wipe"? Hadn't he subjected them to examination under the binocular microscope? Hadn't he checked them out with his own naked eye? Who knew more about what transpired that night in room 253 than Special Investigator Allen G. Smith? And he said "the shirt would not have been within thirty-six inches of the muzzle if that weapon were fired at that shirt."

At once, they were all experts in the jury room. "If it had happened the way she said it did," one juror observed, "we would have expected to see more substantial powder burns."

Another said, "There should have been powder burns on the flesh or shirt or someplace."

And another commented, "Special Investigator Smith's tests showed the gun had to be at least thirty-six inches away, and that meant she had to be standing on the ceiling to shoot him. So she must have had that figured out well ahead of time."

They tried to figure it out, too. Although they were not permitted to deliberate or even to mention the case outside the jury room, some of them took turns that night in the Ramada Inn lying on a double bed and reenacting what one of them described as "what was said at the trial and how she reached over to get the gun, the angle of the bullet and all of that." Somehow they couldn't get their reenactment to match up to Powell's story. They agreed that she was lying. The next morning immediately after breakfast they returned to the jury room, and twenty minutes later they counted up their first official ballot: guilty, by a unanimous vote, of second-degree murder.

They returned to the courtroom a little after ten o'clock, and as Bernadette Powell, standing perfectly still at the defense table, stared at him, foreman Caesar George announced the verdict. Judge Dean explained to Powell that under the law she could not be released on bail, and the bailiffs took her out of the courtroom, down the stairs, across the parking lot, back to Tompkins County Jail.

There she remained for three months, until on June 29 the bailiffs brought her back to the courtroom to stand before Judge Dean and be sentenced for second-degree murder. The lawyers skirmished for ten minutes over legal technicalities she did not understand, and then Judge Dean turned to her.

"How about you, Miss Powell? Do you have anything to say as to sentence?"

"Yes, I do."

In jail, with time to reflect upon her trial and her conviction, she had written out what she wanted to say and asked Allerton to correct her mistakes and type it up. Now, still wearing like a talisman her big silver cross, she stood up at the defendant's table holding in her hands (which did not appear to tremble) two typewritten pages. In a calm, purposeful voice she read out her speech.

> Your Honour, I maintain my innocence. I never plotted to kill my ex-husband, nor did I ever purchase a gun in my entire life. First of all, I do not know Al Smith, and before the trial I never believed a man named Al Smith existed. I thought he was an imaginary person made up by the prosecutor for the sole purpose of getting me to plea bargain. When I saw that the prosecutor had actually gotten a man to say he sold me a gun, I became ill. I cannot explain the actions of Mr. Smith and others who testified against me. It has been said by the prosecution that these people testifying against me were my friends. No, Your Honour, these people were not my friends.
>
> It has been said by the prosecution to put no thought of the child in your mind. I say it is devoid of human feelings to separate an only child from his mother on the

word of a suspected rapist; wife beater and suspected gun
dealer; the emotionally unstable and obvious friends of
my ex-husband, at the risk of my son's mental and physical well being. The prosecution has succeeded in taking
away from me the house I was buying, my job with IBM,
my friends and relatives and my only son.

Your Honour, in the prosecutor's opening statement
to the jury I felt his conduct was contrary to justice. I felt
his power to influence was in violation of acting in ac-
cordance with truth. In the prosecutor's cross examining
questions directed to me, Your Honour, I was questioned
about incidents involving people I did not and do not
know; people that the prosecution did not produce. I was
questioned about welfare fraud. I feel this served as an
influence in mentally manipulating the jurors' minds, and
served to discredit me. I have never committed welfare
fraud. My only desire is to live productively and raise my
son. Instead I face the possibility that I will not be able
to do so. I face the possibility of losing years of my life—
years that would have been prosperous and beneficial to
my son and myself.

In a women's prison it is said that you are stooped to
a mechanical mummy. Prison is said to be for rehabili-
tation. Your Honour, I have nothing to be rehabilitated
from. I am able and capable of functioning within society
without menace. I feel this conviction of murder has been
a serious injustice.

It has been said by the prosecution to arrive at a verdict
you will not be sorry for later. I say, how can you not be
sorry and be comfortable when you know you're taking
years of a human being's life on conflicting evidence. It
is written, In God We Trust. To those jurors who believe
this, then why not believe also, Judge not so ye not be
judged.

At this time, Your Honour, I would like to thank the
people who have contributed to my future defense and
freedom.

Last, Your Honour, it has been said by the prosecution

to show no sympathy toward Miss Powell. Your Honour, I never wanted sympathy. I just wanted justice. I appeal to your court to show actions without severity, and review alternatives with interest, concern, and human regard.

When she finished, Judge Dean pronounced the sentence, the minimum the law allowed for a second-degree murder conviction—fifteen years to life. She would not be eligible for parole until she had served the full fifteen years, and she might be held in prison until she died.

# CHAPTER 8

# APPEAL

Bernadette Powell disappeared behind bars. By rights she should have disappeared from the public eye altogether, like most convicted criminals—out of sight, out of mind. Her attorney wanted nothing more to do with the case. Her family didn't have the know-how or the money to help her. Convicted, locked up, cut off, she could not help herself. There the case would have ended if Powell's crime had not coincided so precisely with the quickening consciousness of the community. Those who took an interest in her set in motion the machinery to free her, and Powell, for her part, urged them on. Behind bars, invisible, she waited while the machine, powered by others, ground on.

In February 1977 the Ithaca *New Times*, Ithaca's alternative newspaper, first reported a new local effort to help battered women: a "task force under the aegis of the Suicide Prevention and Crisis Service . . . looking into the possibilities for emergency shelter for a woman and her children when she is victimized by her mate." (In Tompkins County the official policy of the sheriff's office was not to remove the battering "mate" from the home by arrest, but to "patch things up"—so it was the women and children who had to flee.)

A year and a half later, when Rebecca Allerton, a member of that incipient task force, visited Bernadette Powell in jail, she found a battered woman in deep trouble, just the sort of woman the task force was designed to help, though ideally they might have come across her a little earlier in the dismal, downward gyre of violence, before Herman Smith lay dead. Members of the task force and of Suicide Prevention helped raise money for Powell's bail. By the time she appeared for trial in March 1979 the Tompkins County Task Force on Battered Women had begun to write its name with capital letters, received $5,000 from an anonymous donor, opened a small office on the Ithaca commons, and given Allerton the only paid job ($150 a week) as director. They hoped to get the city's help in establishing a shelter, although Major Edward J. Conley opposed the idea. "Most people in Ithaca," he said, did not "view battered women as a monstrous problem." Allerton, in a letter to the Ithaca *Journal*, insisted the problem was a real one: in 1978 the task force had received 155 calls for help from battered women (including the wives of prosecution witness Al Smith and District Attorney Joe Joch).

In March Allerton received permission from the task force board of directors to attend Bernardette Powell's trial. Needed at Galbraith's law office or the jail or the courthouse, Allerton was less and less to be found at her desk. She let the office go until the morning after Powell was found guilty and locked up again in jail. Then she went back alone, still stunned, to start making phone calls, trying to find some help for Bernadette Powell, who was no longer just a battered woman but now a convicted murderer. Drawn in by the pathos of Powell's story, the urgency and the immensity of her need, Allerton, who knew as well as anyone the needs of all battered women in Tompkins County, became an advocate for this one.

It was all right with Allerton if Galbraith didn't want to appeal the case—she could think of plenty of things he *might* have said to the jury—but it left her with the problem of finding a new attorney. She called Elizabeth Schneider, one of the founders of the Women's Self-Defense Law Project, a program to assist the legal defense of women who are charged with a crime as a result of having defended themselves against violent attack, usually battering or rape. The project's attorneys, Schneider said, were far too busy gathering information and advising attorneys all over the country to take on the Powell case. Why not ask Marty Stolar?

That was a name Allerton had heard before—from other lawyers she'd asked for recommendations. Martin Stolar was a New York City attorney, a former president of the New York National Lawyers Guild, widely known as a first-rate criminal defense lawyer and a champion of radical, unpopular, and sometimes hopeless causes. On April 10, Allerton called him at the office of his firm—then Stolar, Alterman, and Gulielmetti—and in fifteen minutes sketched out the case for him, then mailed him a mimeographed case summary she had spent days preparing.

On May 12 Stolar flew to Ithaca to meet Powell in Tompkins County Jail. Like Allerton, he was drawn to Powell— her innocent wide eyes, her courage, her terror almost palpable in the narrow cell. And the case tantalized him. He could have won it at trial, he was convinced, and he would win it on appeal—for ten thousand dollars. Some circumspect women on the task-force board hesitated to take on that financial obligation, but on June 7, 1979, after thrashing it out among themselves, they signed an agreement with Stolar, Alterman, and Gulielmetti providing that a new group, the Bernadette Powell Defense Fund, would be constituted and would assume all legal and financial responsibility.

Allerton was already preoccupied with fund raising. She and Pat Valls, public education specialist for the task force, peppered the Ithaca *Journal* with letters denouncing the verdict and appealing for contributions. They sent out a press release with a summary of the case, and as a result articles began to appear in the alternative press, in *Aegis*, *No More Cages*, and *The New Women's Times*. They arranged a call-in radio talk show and an interview for the Ithaca *New Times*. Allerton asked always for two things—justice, and the money to secure it.

Others wrote to the Ithaca *Journal* expressing sympathy for Powell and surprise at the verdict. One correspondent, a woman from the outlying town of Trumansburg, wrote in April to raise serious questions which, in the years to follow, were not answered but did not go away.

> There is such a strong sanction for the use of physical force by the majority of males in this society it may be difficult for them to understand/comprehend the experience of the battered wife. In legal cases similar to Ms. Powell's it might do well to know something of the background and attitudes of males who are involved in the trial—whether they are judge, prosecutor or jurors. What if the experiences of the men involved in such court proceedings were ones of physical abuse/violence toward their wives or women friends? Wouldn't they try to justify, consciously or subconsciously, their behavior by minimizing the credibility of the defendant's horrible experiences? This is certainly something to think about.

And indeed it was. Rebecca Allerton had thought about it during the trial, when the district attorney asked Powell with a leer in his voice whether her sex life had been "normal," whether she hadn't enjoyed the battering and torture, whether that wasn't precisely how she got her kicks. Allerton had thought about it ever since she went to Tompkins County Family Court a month before Powell's trial to lend moral support during divorce proceedings to a task-force client— Marie DeJong-Joch. She had married Joe Joch in 1970, before he became district attorney, separated from him in 1977, and charged him with cruel and inhuman treatment. She took the witness stand and, under oath, described—blow by blow—her life as the battered wife of the district attorney. His violent behavior sent Marie DeJong-Joch repeatedly to the doctor, to a therapist, to a lawyer, and finally into court, where the divorce was granted on February 12, 1979, and she was awarded custody of the two boys, the "minor issue" of her fragile and dangerous alliance with Joseph Joch. (Joch did not appear in court to respond to the allegations or to contest the divorce.)

Allerton thought about what she heard in that courtroom, and she told Marty Stolar about it. So at the end of June, when Judge Dean was ready to sentence Powell, Stolar (who was tied up in court in New York City) sent his partner Dan Alterman to raise the issue with Judge Dean and to move for a new trial. "We allege, Judge, that the prosecutor's personal life interfered with his judgment and ability to prosecute the case," Alterman said. "The district attorney is a public official. He is elected by the people of New York. And if there are events that occur in his life that would interfere with his ability to fairly try a case . . . then the district attorney was under an obligation . . . to remove himself from the case." Bernadette Powell, Alterman argued, "is entitled to a new trial and entitled to be prosecuted by someone who doesn't have a stake, and someone who is not a defendant in a matrimonial action where the same kind of charges are being heard."

"Do you want to answer that, Mr. Joch?" Judge Dean asked, peering down from the bench.

Alterman's allegations were "plainly outrageous," Joch snapped. He refused to "dignify them with a remark," and Judge Dean, after quibbling irritably with Alterman about the particular rubric of the New York State Penal Law under which his new trial motion should fall, hurried on to the business at hand. He listened with rising impatience as Bernadette Powell read her prepared statement, called sharply for order when her supporters in the courtroom applauded, and then sentenced her to fifteen years to life. Dan Alterman was still protesting when the bailiffs led her away.

That left Rebecca Allerton to figure out how to raise ten thousand dollars to pay Marty Stolar's firm. In August Judge

Dean turned down Stolar's request that a transcript of the trial be provided to Bernadette Powell, an indigent defendant, at county expense. A group was working on Powell's behalf to raise money for her appeal, Dean said, so let them also buy a transcript. That, Allerton feared, meant raising another twenty-five hundred dollars. She left her job at the task force, where some complained she hadn't done much since she became involved in the Powell case, and volunteered to chair the Bernadette Powell Defense Fund.

On September 6, 1979, Stolar appeared in Tompkins County Court before Judge Dean (and eighty Powell supporters) to request more time to prepare evidence on the motion for a new trial, a motion to be based on evidence newly discovered, not about Bernadette Powell in particular but about battered women in general—the theory of "learned helplessness." Dean granted the request, and a few days later Powell supporters held a press conference to explain the new evidence.

Anne Brous, a member of the Bernadette Powell Defense Fund and a psychotherapist representing the Women's Counseling Collective, for the first time publicly linked the district attorney's conduct in the courtroom to his personal life. There was "probably a connection," Brous told the assembled reporters, between Joch's personal situation and the questions he threw at Bernadette Powell. In fact, the defense planned to introduce expert testimony from Dr. Clara Mayo, a Boston University psychologist, that Joch's line of questioning was based not on fact but on his own "fantasy." They also planned to present expert testimony from Dr. Lenore Walker, a psychologist who conducted a major study of battered women for the National Institute of Mental Health and developed the theory of learned helplessness. Walker found that women battered at will by abusive men, like laboratory dogs subject to random electric shocks, learned that no plan or power of their own could prevent the blows, and gradually they slouched into hopeless submission. Brous concluded that Powell apparently suffered from such a condition.

In October, while the committee kept up its publicity and fund raising, Marty Stolar appeared in Tompkins County Court to explain the theory of learned helplessness to Judge Dean, who feared it might be "a sort of ramification of not guilty by reason of insanity." Stolar assured him that it was not. It was merely "new evidence" that could change the jury's verdict. Walker's expert testimony would show that although Herman Smith apparently had not battered Powell for more than a year before his death, her "psychological state of mind" remained the same. She had been so thoroughly "conditioned" during four years of "brutal marriage" that when Herman abducted her she was thrown back instantly into her old terror, and she became "psychologically unable to move." Without this explanation, Stolar argued, the jurors could not understand why Powell had not simply run away. Her behavior seemed so "completely abnormal" that "the district attorney was able to argue very forcefully and crucially . . . that her story was not credible." Yet the theory of learned helplessness made Powell's conduct understandable and, if presented to a jury, as Dr. Walker herself was prepared to do, would produce "in a minute . . . a verdict less than murder."

Stolar found a second compelling reason for Judge Dean to set aside the verdict—the "misconduct" of the prosecutor. District Attorney Joch, Stolar said, had suggested through his questions that Powell enjoyed being beaten and that she and her attorney, Dorothy Wager, conspired together to "squeeze" Herman Smith for a property settlement. Joch insinuated that Powell invited the violence against her, and implied that her invitation *justified* the violence she suffered. In effect, public official Joch publicly condoned the crime of physical assault. For that reason Stolar asked not only for a new trial but for the appointment of a special prosecutor, independent of Joch's office, who could fairly represent the concern of the people of the state of New York for justice.

"Absurd!" countered Assistant District Attorney John Sherman, representing the prosecution. This theory of learned helplessness wasn't strictly speaking what the law meant by "new evidence," he argued, reverting again to technical niceties of the law. Besides, the Walker theory existed at the time of Powell's trial, so according to the law it was too late to introduce it now; and since it wouldn't change the verdict anyway, it couldn't even be considered by the court. As to the charges of prosecutorial misconduct, Sherman said, Mr. Joch had only been doing his duty, and in any event, it was up to the appellate court to decide whether misconduct had occurred. "Let him argue that upon appeal," Sherman said. "That's what appeals are for."

As Judge Dean took the defense motion under consideration, popular support for Powell continued to grow in the community and beyond. Actress Maureen Garrett, who played in the television soap opera "The Guiding Light" the role of a raped and battered wife sentenced to twelve years for killing her husband, visited Bernadette Powell in the Tompkins County Jail, held a press conference to express her support, and talked about the case in an interview printed in *Soap Opera Digest*. "I'm just playing a role," she said, "but Powell's case is frighteningly real." Activist Angela Davis, addressing Cornell students in November, described Powell as a victim of racist society and of her husband, now being victimized again by the criminal justice system.

The Ithaca *Journal*, which first discovered the plight of battered women in a series of articles published only three years before, editorialized:

> We are not legal experts enough to judge whether Stoler's arguments should be aired in a new trial or in an appeal. Nor can we judge whether the jury convicted Powell of murder because she was misunderstood and demeaned by stereotypes, or because the prosecution discredited her

story with contrary evidence. But Stoler is certainly right that we should reassess our thinking, both in and out of the courtroom, about battered women. . . . It's time we stopped excusing violence within the family by insinuating that the victims asked for it. It's time we throw away the stereotypes that battered women enjoy being brutalized, and realize that they bear emotional as well as physical scars.

The Cornell student newspaper, the *Sun*, took a much stronger stand in a special column about the Powell case: "For an accused wife beater to prosecute a battered wife is inexcusable. To believe for one moment that the personal life of the district attorney did not interfere with his ability to perform his duty impartially is a farce."

In December, riding the crest of public opinion, the Bernadette Powell Defense Fund netted thirty-two hundred dollars at a benefit auction of goods and services donated by Powell's well-wishers, and her story hit the front page of the *Village Voice*. More than 650 Ithacans signed letters to Judge Dean urging that she be granted a new trial. As 1979 ended, Powell was still in Tompkins County Jail awaiting Judge Dean's decision. But her star was rising.

Then, on January 15, 1980, Judge Dean denied Powell's motion for a new trial. The "new evidence"—the expert psychological testimony Stolar wanted to introduce—"would not change the result" of the trial, he wrote in his decision. And he was "of the opinion that the District Attorney's personal life did not affect his performance as an officer of this Court." Joch's cross-examination on "female myths (such as defendant's potential enjoyment in being beaten by deceased)" amounted to no more than "harmless errors." And one could argue, Dean wrote, "that the District Attorney had a duty" to find out through zealous cross-examination whether Powell "provoked the aggressions of Herman Smith." Like Joch's questioning, Dean's decision suggested that a battered woman might be getting only what she asked for—

one of the very "female myths" Stolar's expert witnesses were intended to refute.

Rebecca Allerton, who had just visited Powell in the Tompkins County Jail, heard the announcement of Dean's decision on her car radio and returned to the jail to break the news to Powell. (Later she complained to the press, "They didn't have the common courtesy to tell her. They expected this woman to hear about the rest of her life from a top-forty radio station.") Terrified of going to prison, Powell lost altogether the power to speak, so for what seemed a very long time she and Allerton sat together in silence, holding hands. The next day Powell was led from the jail in handcuffs and driven downstate to the Bedford Hills Correctional Facility, New York State's maximum-security prison for women. There she moved through her new life in perfect silence, and because she still suffered from the claustrophobia that began to haunt her when Herman locked her in the trunk of her car, she slept each night on the floor of her cell with her face pressed to the crack of light beneath the door.

The next day Marty Stolar announced that he would appeal Powell's conviction, but he was still waiting for a transcript of the trial. For months odd bits of the record had been delivered piecemeal to the offices of Stolar, Alterman, and Gulielmetti, like serialized chapters of a Victorian novel printed in the wrong order. In August Stolar received Dorothy Wager's testimony, District Attorney Joch's cross-examination of Bernadette Powell, and a bill for $150.75. A week later Joch's summation arrived with a bill for $54.75. On March 31, 1980, a little over a year after Bernadette Powell was convicted of murder, two and a half months after Judge Dean denied Powell a new trial, the remaining pieces of her trial transcript were delivered, and Stolar, who had taken the case on the strength of Powell and Allerton's account of the proceedings, saw for the first time a complete record of the trial.

Then, for months, he and legal intern Jeff Stein, a student at New York University Law School, pored over the transcript in search of "reversible error" in trial procedure and assembled a brief for the appellate court. That court, which decides whether a defendant was given a "fair trial," evaluates fairness not in terms of the facts of the case or moral standards or common sense, but in terms of a set of rules, precedents, procedures, and traditions so convoluted and arcane that they cannot be set down in plain English. At last, on December 29, 1980, Stolar submitted his brief, and in March 1981 Justice Ann T. Mikol, the only woman on the appellate bench, granted permission for an additional appeal of the new trial motion denied by Judge Dean to be consolidated with the appeal of Powell's conviction and heard by the court in June 1981.

Stolar had found many violations of proper procedure in the conduct of Powell's trial, and he set out these "reversible errors" in his appeal brief as straightforwardly as legal prose permits. Powell was "denied a fair trial," he argued, "by the cumulative prejudicial misconduct of the District Attorney," who not only shored up his case with "racial stereotypes" and "false inferences and unfounded myths about battered women" but also presented as though it were true "a crucial fact" for which there was *no* evidence, namely, the allegation that Powell stabbed Herman Smith at the Cadillac Lounge. These and other technical violations were the "overzealous actions and arguments of a prosecutor bent on conviction at any cost," Stolar argued, and the reason for this misconduct lay in the district attorney's "personal life crisis which affected his ability to properly discharge his duties" and which should have caused him "to recuse himself" from conducting the prosecution.

Stolar also heaped errors upon "the Court," that is, Judge Dean. He argued that the court should not have admitted evidence about Powell's fight with the bottle-throwing Jimmy McNeil or her dubious welfare applications, evidence that had nothing to do with the crime charged against Powell and merely served to prejudice the jury against her. Nor should the court have allowed Investigator Allen G. Smith to offer "without foundation" an expert "scientific" opinion on the firing distance of the gun, particularly when his observations were incomplete, his tests inadequate, and his expertise in another field—matching bullets to guns, not fabric and powder burns. Finally, Stolar argued, the court's instructions to the jury were inadequate and thoroughly confusing. Dean gave the jury only a partial definition of "justification"—crucial to Powell's defense—and didn't explain how it applied to Powell's case. And his baffling definition of "reasonable doubt" left jurors the mistaken impression they could disregard evidence and decide the case on the basis of how they "felt" about it.

Stolar's second brief, appealing Judge Dean's denial of Powell's new trial motion, also wrestled with fine points of law rather than the facts of the case. Most important was the question whether "scientifically based expert testimony of a battered woman's mental status, perceptions and reactions" could be defined as "newly discovered evidence" under New York State law. The other questions raised in the brief—such as whether the "court below erred . . . by misapplying CPL 440.30 in denying the motion without a hearing"—were legal technicalities having much to do with Powell's fate but nothing to do with what happened between two estranged people in a motel room in the small hours of July 9, 1978.

In May, Joch filed a reply brief with the court contending that the trial had been eminently fair and his own conduct above reproach. "No disqualifying 'personal' interest is present," he wrote, using the curiously backhanded phrasing of legal jargon. And as prosecutor, he argued, he was entitled to put Herman Smith's assaults on Powell "in their proper perspective." They were "sexually motivated," Joch contended, "at least on Herman's part and perhaps acquiesced in to some degree by Powell," and because "these acts were sexually motivated on his part," Joch argued, "regardless of her acquiescence or lack of it, . . . they are not any proof of his violence toward her or of any reasonable fear on her part of serious physical injury at his hands."

That argument, that violence against a woman, against her will, if committed in the name of sex, was not *real* violence, seemed a peculiar view for a district attorney to take, and for his constituents who might be victims of sex crimes and assault, a particularly dangerous one. It alarmed authorities on women's self-defense law, including law professor Elizabeth Schneider, who filed as an *amicus curiae* a brief on Powell's behalf, arguing that Joch's conduct was indeed "improper and prejudicial" and that his failure to step out of the case "denied Bernadette Powell's rights to a fair trial." Schneider's fifty-page brief was endorsed by the Center for Constitutional Rights, the NAACP, the National Center on Women and Family Law, the New York State Coalition Against Domestic Violence, the Tompkins County Task Force for Battered Women, the Aid for Women Victims of Violence, and other organizations.

Rebecca Allerton, even as she issued news releases about the appeal and wrote to organizations, asking their help as signatories to Schneider's brief, wondered how anyone could possibly make sense of the law. "I thought the appellate judges would just want to know that Bernadette is not a murderer," she complained to a law professor interested in Powell's case. "But instead we have to give them all these technical legal questions. Who cares?"

"Don't be fooled," the professor cautioned. "Judges like to look like legal geniuses, but really they just go over the summary of the case and figure out whether they think the defendant is guilty or not. If they think she's *not* guilty, they'll make up some technical reason to reverse the decision. If they think she *is* guilty, forget it."

The appellate court allotted Stolar just twenty minutes to present his oral argument and refused altogether to hear from Elizabeth Schneider, even when Stolar offered to share his time with her. His case was difficult to make, and touchy, for in part it called upon the five gray-haired men of the court to censure one of their own. If they did so, deciding that D.A. Joch had acted improperly, they would set a precedent: they would establish more rigorous standards of fairness for the legal brotherhood of which they were a part, the brotherhood that accorded them eminence. But in the midst of Stolar's delicate argument, one gray head went up, and the justice, interrupting in mid-sentence, demanded, "Wasn't there some evidence that she bought the gun?"

"Yes, there was," Stolar conceded, "but our contention is that . . ."

"Didn't the court hear testimony from a man who sold her the gun?" the justice persisted.

"Miss Powell denied that she bought the gun, but the point to be made here is that . . ."

But the point to be made had already become irrelevant, even to Allerton, seated in the second row. They think she did it, she said to herself. They think she bought the gun. They aren't even listening.

On July 24, 1981, a little more than three years after the death of Herman Smith, the appellate court announced its decision upholding the conviction of Bernadette Powell. "We have considered all of the defendant's other contentions," the court said, "and fail to find prejudicial issues." As to Joch's improper cross-examination, the court ruled that if the defense introduces evidence of "a victim's violent temperament" to show "a state of mind which justified the defendant's actions" then the prosecution should have "a fair opportunity to dispute defendant's contention by vigorous cross-examination." Whether or not Joch should have stepped out of the case because of his personal concerns, the court did not say. The decision of the five justices was unanimous.

Allerton was baffled. "I just don't get it. How come we have to have this elaborate technical question of law to go before the court, and then when we get there they don't pay any attention to it? How come they say they deal in matters

of law, not fact, and then the only thing they consider is
their version of the facts?" To the press she said only that
"the Bernadette Powell Defense Fund is extremely unhappy
with the decision of the appellate division. We plan to take
the case to the Court of Appeals hoping that there justice
will finally be served."

Exultant, Joch told reporters that "Powell received one
of the fairest trials I have ever seen." It is "inappropriate,"
he said, "to use the jury system to argue broad social issues.
The appellate division kept its eye on the real issues and
dealt with the guilt or innocence of the defendant." Powell,
he said, was simply using the issue of battered women to
hide a premeditated murder, and her misguided supporters
"picked the wrong horse to back."

Joe Joch could afford to crow. He had weathered some
bad press, including a series of articles about him in the
Cornell *Sun* just after the Powell conviction. JOCH ALLEG-
EDLY BEAT EX-WIFE one headline read, and RAPE VICTIMS
CALL D. A. JOCH HARSH. But despite the wife-beating allegations, he'd come off looking better than Judge Dean,
who, as the *Sun* reported, habitually let sex offenders go.
(Dean turned loose the rapist of a sixteen-year-old-girl with
a fine for "sexual misconduct," and he let a particularly
brutal rape-murderer plead to manslaughter and then released him altogether on a technicality.) In the *Sun* exposé
Dirk Galbraith looked bad, too. "Rape is a very subjective
thing," he was quoted as saying. "There is a gray area: the
male has one thing on his mind; the female has another
thing on her mind. They disagree on the facts later." Still
the publicity hurt Joch, and for the time being at least he
let go of his hopes of a judgeship. Instead on June 5, 1981,
just a few days after he filed his brief in reply to Powell's
appeal, Joch announced that he would run for a third term
as district attorney.

Meanwhile, Marty Stolar applied to Justice Jacob Fuchsberg of the New York State Court of Appeals for permission
to appeal the decision of the appellate division. He was

confidant Justice Fuchsberg would take an interest in the appeal because it rested upon an extension of the concept of "prosecutorial misconduct" set forth in the case of *People* v. *Zimmer*, a case in which only the year before Justice Fuchsberg himself had written the decision. Joch, in the midst of his reelection campaign, filed an opposing memo with the Court of Appeals.

On November 3, Republican Ben Bucko, who had practiced law privately in the little town of Groton since 1968 and had no prosecutorial experience, upset Democrat Joe Joch by a margin of six hundred votes. "Bucko must have won over some Democrats and independents," the *Journal* reported, and speculation held that those swing voters were women. The outgoing mayor stated flatly that Joch lost because of his "prosecution of the Bernadette Powell case," and Joch himself told reporters, "No doubt about it—it didn't help." He claimed that Powell's appeal had been delayed intentionally to coincide with his election campaign "in order to create the maximum amount of political embarrassment to me."

Ten days later Justice Fuchsberg, finding "no significant question of law" in the Powell case, denied permission to appeal to the state Court of Appeals. In December Stolar asked the court to reconsider, and at the end of January 1982, Justice Fuchsberg denied the motion. Powell's supporters had exhausted their recourse to the courts of the state of New York.

Bernadette Powell remained in the "correctional facility" at Bedford Hills. She promised God that if he would restore her speech she would try to live a decent life. God complied, and Powell ran for office in the prison chapter of the NAACP (narrowly losing out for president), studied for an associate's degree in sociology and psychology, and qualified to live on the honors floor, which housed only exemplary prisoners. She tried, for the sake of her son and her supporters, to keep her spirits up, but when the Court of Appeals refused to hear her case she felt herself sliding toward despair. She had refused all along to join the Long Termers Club at the prison, unwilling to admit that she might be there for more than a few months. But already she had been in prison for years, and since the courts declined to hear her case, there she would have to remain for seven and a half years before she could apply for gubernatorial clemency, which almost never was granted, or fifteen years before she could apply for parole. She tasted a bitterness that others could not know.

Then, in April 1982, she received a letter written out in schoolgirl script much like her own. It was a cautious, painstaking letter that began, "Dear Burnadette, You do not know of me but I know of you through your husband. . . ."

# CHAPTER 9

# NEW EVIDENCE

"But can't you remember what it said, Bernadette?" Ann Cedarholm asked.

"Naw," Powell replied, staring vacantly past her visitor at the chain link and razor-wire fences outside the window. "Just what I said. Just that Herman bought the gun."

"But, Bernadette, you must know how important that is!" Ann Cedarholm was by nature a patient woman and by profession a psychiatric nurse, but there were times when Powell tried her to the limit. Enlisted as a Powell supporter by her daughter Carol, an early member of the Bernadette Powell Defense Fund, Ann Cedarholm dutifully drove ten miles from her home in Katonah to Bedford Hills prison to visit Bernadette Powell almost every weekend. At first she believed, as Carol and Rebecca Allerton told her, that Powell would not be in prison very long; but Powell's appeal failed and she stayed on at Bedford Hills. Ann Cedarholm, not knowing how to stop, went on visiting week after week, even when Powell kept her waiting for an hour while she dressed, even when Powell handed her lists of clothes she had to have, even when Powell merely sat and smoked and stared at the wall, brooding angrily, as she did one day in April, about the failure of her lawyers.

"It's just the same thing I've been saying all along," Powell said listlessly. "I put the letter in the mail to Marty. He's so smart, let him figure it out."

"But Bernadette, who was it from? Do you remember the name?"

"Naw. Just some woman. Let Marty do some work for a change." She lit another king-size Kool off the one in her hand and jammed out the butt in the tin ashtray. She blew the smoke at the window.

Two months earlier, when the appeals court had refused to hear her case, Powell dropped her college studies and started research on constitutional law in the prison's small law library. She drafted a long paper on the violation of her constitutional rights under the Fourth Amendment and the Fifth, the Sixth, the Eighth, the Fourteenth. Stolar, she said, should be arguing for her release on grounds of these violations, and while Stolar vainly explained his own legal strategy to her in long, careful letters, Powell fumed.

It took Ann Cedarholm one phone call to learn that Marty Stolar had never received the mysterious letter, and another phone call to summon Rebecca Allerton from Ithaca.

"Maybe her name started with an S, or Sh," Powell told Allerton. "She said Herman bought the gun."

Allerton convinced her that the letter must be found. "If it says what you think it says, Marty might be able to use it to get you out of here."

"He doesn't give a damn about me."

"Look, Bernadette, I understand you're pissed about being here, but you've got the wrong guy. Marty didn't put you here. He's the one who's trying to get you out."

"He doesn't care about me. All he cares about is himself. He's just in it for the fame and the money."

"Fame and money! Out of *this* case? You've got some paranoid imagination." Allerton paused, worn out. "Just find the letter, Bernadette. Find the letter."

A few days later Powell telephoned Ann Cedarholm. The letter, she said, had turned up in the mail room at the prison.

She had slipped it into an envelope addressed to Marty
Stolar, but because she neglected to write down her return
address and prison number, the mail room didn't send it
out. Within two hours Cedarholm had collected the letter
at the prison and driven with it to Marty Stolar's office in
lower Manhattan.

Laboriously written out on lined paper, like an exercise
in penmanship, it said:

Dear Burnadette,

You do not know of me but I know of you through your
husband. I read your story in the Binghamton newspaper
and let me just say I was puzzled to read that some one
said they sold you a gun. I know this cannot be true and
I just want you to know that I believe every word you
said because if you remember a day that you brought
your son to Herman's house to go fishing one morning
and you saw a bunch of us sleeping on the floor and you
called the police on us. Well Herman was planning to kill
you then. He told all of us. I was his main girl (I don't
mean to hurt you). I just want you to know the truth even
though it is to late.

Anyway one night we went to Ithaca and Herman and
I went to this girls apartment. The girl opened the door
and said that you were at work at I.B.M. and Herman
was playing with your son. Anyway this guy by the name
of Smitty, Herman called him came over. The girl went
in or down her hall and we heard a loud noise and she
came and told us the gun went off in her room. She gave
the gun to Smitty and he told Herman something about
scratches on the gun. I was playing with your son but I
heard them. The girl also gave Smitty a bag and later on
our drive back to Binghamton I saw that it was some
bullets so I know Herman bought a gun but I really did
not believe he was going to kill you because he told me
about somebody who once put his son in the hospital.

Anyway Burnadette, I did not know that all of this
happened to you because I went with a guy who use to

beat me to so I understand. Herman use to drink a lot just like my old man. My old man never knew I use to hang with Herman though. I would have never known until I read the paper. I wish I could help you. I know your innocent because its impossible I think for both of you to have the same gun. Man! the police are crazy. Burnadette this sounds jive but pray to God. I do. Keep the faith.

It was signed in the same careful script: *Cynthia Shuford.*

Stolar put in a call to Henry Radke, an upstate private investigator. To Powell he sent a note expressing "cautious optimism" at the possibility of new evidence, and once again she grew angry. Stolar was going to "mess up," she wrote to Allerton. Stolar was out to "ruin" her. She thought the Shuford letter could be sent immediately to Judge Dean who, once he read that the gun belonged, after all, to Herman, would simply order her release from prison. She couldn't understand why Stolar and Allerton still said, "We have a long way to go."

Allerton wrote to reassure her and to explain that first the defense team had to *find* Cynthia Shuford. "We have to make sure that she'll cooperate, sign an affidavit, be willing to testify. She may not, she may split town, she may be a complete basket case—a nut. We still don't know what we're dealing with."

The Shuford letter, postmarked in Binghamton, bore a return address on Oak Street, but investigator Radke quickly learned that Shuford didn't really live there. The address was that of a woman who had taken her in as a foster child in 1974, when she was fifteen. A few months later Shuford disappeared, and the police marked her down as a runaway until she turned up two years later in the protective custody of Pennsylvania police after they arrested the man who had abducted her and forced her into prostitution. She had a child, and later, back in Binghamton, she bore another one. She couldn't take care of them—she was still so much a child herself—so her foster mother took them in. Cynthia came around once a week or so to pick up her welfare check and to see how they were getting on. From official sources Radke learned that Shuford was a twenty-two-year-old "mulatto" with no employment and no criminal convictions.

Radke left his phone number and Stolar's and Rebecca Allerton's, but Shuford didn't call back. Allerton wrote to her at the Oak Street address, but Shuford didn't answer the letter. Then Allerton thought of Powell's brother, Oscar Lee, the closest thing in Binghamton to a hip disco DJ. If Shuford spent any time hanging around the local night spots, there was just a chance that Oscar Lee might know who she was. But Oscar Lee too kept his address a secret, so Allerton left a message for him with his mother. Yes, he said, when he returned the call, there was some girl he'd seen around who he thought might be named Cynthia. If he ran into her again, he'd ask her to call Allerton.

Two days later Cynthia called. She agreed to meet Allerton and Radke on the steps of the old courthouse in downtown Binghamton. The place was public, anonymous, and at two o'clock Saturday afternoon almost certain to be deserted. But not that Saturday. Grouped in the center of the steps, the high school band, all polished brass and gold braid, struck up "My Baby Was a Centerfold" while cheerleaders beat out the rhythm with tattered pompoms and masses of people roared. It was a rally for the Binghamton Whalers soccer team. "When they make the movie," Allerton said, "this will be a great scene."

Radke didn't laugh. "Just look for a woman who's not happy about being here," he said.

They found her, and the next day Radke sent off a report of the meeting to Stolar:

On May 15, 1982, at about 2:30 P.M., contact was made with Cynthia Shuford in front of the Broome County Court House in Binghamton, NY. Cynthia was interviewed in the Midtown Mall opposite the courthouse.

Cynthia was nervous and wanted to leave from the moment she sat down with H. Radke and R. Allerton. Cynthia expressed some fear of getting into trouble over the interview and needed constant reassurance. . . . Cynthia would not give her address to R. Allerton or H. Radke but agreed to another meeting, stating she would sign a statement.

Three days later, on May 19, Dan Alterman flew to Binghamton to meet Radke, Allerton, and the elusive Cynthia Shuford. There, in a coffee shop in the Midtown Mall, Cynthia Shuford signed an affidavit.

On May 28 Stolar submitted to the Tompkins County Court another notice of a motion to vacate judgment. "New evidence has been discovered," he advised the court, "which could not have been produced by the defendant at the trial and which is of such character as to create a probability that had such evidence been received at the trial the verdict would have been more favorable to the defendant."

So, on July 9, 1982, four years to the day since the death of Herman Smith, Bernadette Powell once again sat quietly in an Ithaca courtroom while others presented testimony and arguments that would decide the course of her life. She had grown thinner and more stylish. She wore a smart pale linen dress with a brown linen jacket and high-heeled shoes, a costume Allerton had picked out at the Ithaca Thrift Shop. She had abandoned the big silver cross, just as sometime during the last years at Bedford Hills she had mislaid her Christian faith. She could no longer believe it was God who mapped out her life.

Almost everything else had changed too, as if to emphasize to Powell how handily the world went on without her. It almost seemed that the only constant in the world was her own imprisonment. She sat now in a different courtroom in a different courthouse, a cavernous space in an old building, so thoroughly refurbished it resembled a suburban church. On the bench sat William Barrett, another Cornellian, law-school class of 1963, former alderman and school-board member, and for years an appointed city judge, until he ran in 1980 as a Democrat for the judgeship vacated by Bruce Dean, who retired reluctantly at the mandatory age of seventy. At the prosecutor's table sat Joe Joch's successor, Ben Bucko, a tweedy, pipe-smoking fellow who covered his ineptitude with affability. For the defense, Stolar and the feisty Dan Alterman replaced the well-tailored Mr. Galbraith. Rebecca Allerton was still there, as she had been at Powell's trial, seated behind Powell in the first row, chewing her cuticles. Carol Cedarholm was there, as she had been at the trial, this time with her mother, Ann, beside her. The other hundred or so spectators were new, Ithacans who over the years had grown to sympathize with Powell and who had offered their time or services or money to the Bernadette Powell Defense Fund.

The only witness at the hearing was Cynthia Shuford, who somehow miraculously appeared, as she had said she would. She was a young, heavyset woman, looking eminently respectable in a simple white knit dress and carefully pressed hairdo. Step by step Marty Stolar led her through the story of how she had met Herman Smith in the bar at the Ramada Inn and, from time to time, saw him when she "was out." She knew him well enough to know that he had "a tattoo of a woman on his left breast." She described the pot party at Herman's apartment interrupted by Powell's arrival, and Herman's anger after the police had come and gone. She described a trip with Herman to Ithaca, sometime in "the summer of 1978," and a woman who said the gun had gone off in her bedroom, and a guy named Smitty who handed Herman a paper bag containing bullets and a "small gun." She didn't question Herman about his "business." "When he drank all the time," she said, "I knew, you know, I assumed he'd get violent, so I didn't question him on anything."

She explained also why she had not come forward before.

"In seventy-eight I was young," she said. "I didn't much care about reading the newspaper. I just partied and did that sort of thing. And recently I've become more concerned, since I've gotten older, with what's happening in the news." Until she read the Binghamton Sunday *Press* on March 28, 1982, and saw a feature story on the Powell case headlined SHE KILLED HIM, BUT WAS IT MURDER?, she knew nothing about the death of Herman Smith.

Bucko wanted to bring Al Smith and Diane Nelson to the stand—he had them waiting in the basement of the courthouse—to ask if they had ever seen this Cynthia Shuford. But Stolar argued, and Judge Barrett agreed, that the hearing was designed only to introduce the new evidence, not to try the case all over again.

Instead Judge Barrett asked Stolar to sum up his argument. If Shuford had testified at the trial, Stolar said, "her credibility would have been taken into account by the jury, as well as the credibility of witnesses who said things that were different from her. We would have wound up at the trial with Al Smith and Cynthia Shuford being the only people who testified about seeing a gun. Al Smith testifying he sold it to Bernadette Powell, Cynthia Shuford testifying that Smitty sold the gun . . . to Herman Smith. . . . So, the jury would have been left with a determination as to whether Herman Smith bought the gun or Bernadette Powell bought the gun. . . . Either believing or disbelieving both witnesses, they could have found a reasonable doubt on that and still arrived at a verdict less than murder. . . ."

Then it was over, and Judge Barrett retired. Powell, who had been transferred from Bedford Hills for the hearing, was escorted by a deputy back to Tompkins County Jail. District Attorney Bucko gathered up his papers, pulled out his pipe, and dallied near the door, available to the press, who hurried past him to file their stories. The Powell team—Stolar, Alterman, legal assistant Jeff Stein, Rebecca Allerton, witness Cynthia Shuford, Powell's brother Oscar Lee, and her son—good-humored and confident, riding the crest of the dramatic argument, strolled across the courthouse square to the Moosewood Restaurant for a celebratory lunch.

Only a week later Judge Barrett announced his decision, the first quick decision in the Powell case since the verdict of the jury. In a twenty-two-page document he summarized the facts of the killing, Cynthia Shuford's testimony, the testimony of all the "relevant" trial witnesses—Al Smith, Diane Nelson, Lisa Johnson, Leon Farley, and David Brown—and the testimony of witnesses who "testified Defendant made statements that she wanted to kill or harm her husband."

Faced with the tricky legalistic problem of deciding what qualified as "new evidence" under the New York State Penal Law, Barrett listed the criteria:

> 1. It must be such as will probably change the result if a new trial is granted; 2. It must have been discovered since the trial; 3. It must be such as could not have been discovered before the trial by the exercise of due diligence; 4. It must be material to the issue; 5. It must not be cumulative to the former issue; and, 6. It must not be merely impeaching or contradicting of the former evidence.

When he set Shuford's testimony against these standards, he found that it clearly measured up to three of them: it was literally "new," material to the issue, and couldn't have been discovered before the trial. But that left three more standards to puzzle over. "The questions for decision here," Barrett wrote, "are whether the evidence is impeaching or contradictory of former evidence and whether it 'is of such a character as to create a probability' it would change the verdict if offered at trial." To find the answers he set off on the narrow, tortuous path of legal reasoning.

There was little question, he wrote, that Cynthia Shuford's story about "the transaction with the gun" was "different" from the stories of the prosecution witnesses; and it served to back up Powell's "claim that Herman Smith had the gun." But to accept Shuford's story, Barrett said, the jury would have to discredit Al Smith, Diane Nelson, Lisa Johnson, and David Brown, all of whom testified that Powell and Al Smith were in Diane's apartment when the gun went off. "None of these witnesses were interested parties," Barrett maintained, "and while some attempts were made to attack their credibility, no reason was shown why they would all have a motive for lying." He concluded that the jury had correctly found their testimony "credible and consistent." (Some "minor" discrepancies in their testimony he attributed to "the lapse of time between the events and the trial.")

On the other hand, Barrett had his doubts about Shuford's story. He found certain "questionable" details and noticed in particular "a major inconsistency." Shuford said the gun sale took place in Ithaca "about a week" after Herman's notorious pot party, which Barrett said was held on June 27. But other testimony at the trial, including Powell's, held that Powell had moved to Owego on June 28; and by July 1 her son was staying in Binghamton with Georgia Bowman. "Thus, after June 27," Barrett concluded, "neither the boy nor Defendant would have been at Diane Nelson's apartment." Nor did Shuford's testimony about the pot party correspond to Powell's. Powell had testified that when she arrived at Herman's apartment, he was "asleep and he did not wake up." Shuford, on the other hand, said "she heard Defendant tell Smith she was going to call police."

Consequently, Judge Barrett wrote, "even if this further evidence had been given at trial it is not probable that it would have changed the verdict. . . . I therefore conclude the Defendant's motion should be denied."

Marty Stolar was at first disbelieving, then angry. Rebecca Allerton, equally angry, wrote to the Ithaca *Journal*:

Ms. Shuford's testimony went to the heart of the key issue, namely that of the possession of the gun. Yet Judge Barrett found in this testimony, given four years after the fact, "a major inconsistency" in dating certain incidents; while on the other hand, he charitably attributed gross factual errors in the testimony of prosecution witnesses, given three years ago at the trial, to a simple "lapse of time." If there is inconsistency here, it may be in Judge Barrett's standards of evaluation.

Once again Stolar prepared a brief for the appellate division. Once again he outlined the facts of the case, the content of Shuford's new evidence, and the decision of Judge Barrett. He focused on the main legal issues—"whether it is probable that the testimony would have resulted in a more favorable verdict and whether it was merely 'contradictory' of former evidence." He argued that "the new evidence blows a devastating hole in the prosecution's case, undermines the integrity of the conviction, and creates substantial doubt about whether an innocent woman has been jailed for life."

Once again Stolar set forth all the reasons to doubt the word of the prosecution witnesses—from emotional illness to criminal character—and compared their word to Shuford's. Judge Barrett was wrong to label her testimony "suspect," Stolar said, when all of the "objective criteria" pointed in the opposite direction. And he was wrong in requiring Shuford's testimony to "outweigh all the other evidence" and to change the jury's verdict. The law, Stolar said, required merely that her testimony create a reasonable doubt and make a different verdict "probable." And that much it certainly did. "At the very least, the jury would be faced with a set of facts which is as consistent with innocence as with guilt," Stolar argued, and even if they didn't believe Powell innocent, they couldn't have found "beyond a reasonable doubt, to a moral certainty" that she intentionally killed Herman Smith. They would have reached "a verdict more favorable than murder."

The "discrepancies" in Shuford's testimony Stolar easily explained. The notorious pot party did not take place on

June 27, as the trial record said, but on the preceding Friday night, June 23, as the Endicott Police Department records would prove. (The erroneous date entered the trial record through defense attorney Galbraith, who, according to Stolar's generous construction, "misspoke" at the trial.) Thus, several days elapsed between the pot party and the time of the gun sale, a period "which after a span of four years, could seem like 'about a week later' to the witness." In short, the "major inconsistency" lay in the mistaken trial record and not in Shuford's testimony.

Stolar also explained away the inconsistency between Shuford's account of the pot party and Powell's. Either woman, he said, could easily have been mistaken about whether Smith was awake or asleep. (Considering that Powell was upset and that Shuford had spent the night smoking dope, the discrepancy seemed to Stolar "hardly surprising.") In any case, he argued, "on the important points, that there was such a party, that a number of young people and Smith were there, that Powell threatened to call the police, that the police in fact arrived, and that Smith was extremely angry," both women agreed.

Yet there was still a technical legal issue to be gotten around. Barrett had ruled that Shuford's testimony was "contradictory" of evidence presented at trial and therefore unacceptable under the legal standards he had outlined. Yet the standards also required that new evidence be "material" to the case, and as Stolar argued, if the new evidence were *not* contradictory it probably would not be considered material either. (It is hard to imagine why the defense would trouble to present evidence that *didn't* contradict the prosecution.) The question (as set forth in the language of *People* v. *Salemi*) was whether the new evidence were "*merely* contradictory," and that, Stolar argued, was not the case. "The primary effect of the Shuford testimony," he maintained, "is to provide *new, probative* information—i.e. that Herman Smith purchased the gun with which he was shot. . . . Although the newly discovered evidence has the

effect of being contradictory of some of the evidence ad-
duced at trial, it is only contradictory in secondary conse-
quence."

Stolar's arguments seemed mightily persuasive to the defenders of Bernadette Powell. Yet the decision, and Powell's
life, rested not upon persuasive arguments about the facts
of the case, but upon legalistic definitions and applications
of terms like *probability, probative, contradictory, merely,*
and *new.* Again the defense attorney's reasonable arguments
for justice masked the fact that the decision would rest in
the minds—the experiences, idiosyncrasies, assumptions,
values, blind spots, and biases—of the judges and the construction they put upon legalisms.

On May 31, 1983, after nearly a year of jockeying with
the appellate division for the right to be heard, Marty Stolar
took the train north along the brimming Hudson River to
Albany to argue before five justices of the appellate court.
Seated behind their elevated bench, the justices appeared
bodiless, their heads borne upon the surface as upon a salver,
the ashen heads of four white men, gray and balding, and
of Justice Ann Mikol, blond and stiffly coiffed. Behind them
on the wood-paneled wall was displayed in high relief the
great seal of the State of New York, bearing one figure
holding the scales of justice and another holding a sword.
In the center, over the motto Excelsior was depicted a pas-
toral landscape, over which the sun appeared to be rising,
or perhaps setting.

For the justices, Stolar set forth orally the major arguments written in his brief, edged all the while by a digital
clock built into the lectern, knocking off his allotted fifteen
minutes. In his turn, Ben Bucko, laying aside a houndstooth
tweed cap reminiscent of Sherlock Holmes, argued that the
only real issue in the Powell case was what happened on
the night of the killing. His argument was disingenuous, for
what happened that night must have depended largely upon
which of the two people involved possessed the gun; but

Bucko, ever amiable and obtuse, would not be drawn into that issue.

Stolar's time passed too quickly and then he was back on the train headed downriver to New York City, drinking bourbon in the club car. "How about this rumor that Shuford is Oscar Powell's girl friend?" I asked him.

"I've heard."

"What if you had some evidence that it's true?"

"My client knows nothing about it," he said, "and it's my job as an advocate to represent my client." I bought another round and watched the sun fall to the west of the broad blue river while Stolar went on vigorously, as though he were still addressing the court. "Whatever information you or anybody else might have about Bernadette Powell the *person*, what is important and significant about the Powell *case* is that she didn't get a *fair* trial, in the sense that a black person can't get a fair trial in a system with racist values and attitudes, and a battered woman can't get a fair trial in a system that relies on sexist values and trivializes wife beating. Bernadette's trial and the verdict were based on attitudes and values that should have no place in society at all, let alone in the process by which we take a person's liberty away for life." He was still reasoning with the court, persuading the law to fairness, entreating the system to deliver at last its promised justice for all, when the train dove into darkness under the city, pulling into Grand Central.

He had worn a new tie, a pale yellow silk, for the occasion, but it didn't change his luck, or the system. On July 7, 1983, almost a year after Judge Barrett ruled against Bernadette Powell and the testimony of Cynthia Shuford, just two days short of the fifth anniversary of the death of Herman Smith, the appellate division upheld Judge Barrett's decision and denied leave to appeal to the Court of Appeals.

In September, despite the appellate court's ruling, Stolar applied for leave to appeal to the Court of Appeals. District Attorney Bucko submitted legal papers opposing the move.

Bernadette Powell, awaiting the decision, asked to be transferred back from the upstate minimum-security facility at Albion, where because of her outstanding prison record she had spent the last year, to the larger maximum-security prison at Bedford Hills, which offered more programs for inmates. Powell already had earned an associate's degree at Bedford Hills; now she wanted to go on for a bachelor's degree. That would be a way of doing her time without, as prison parlance has it, letting the time do her. She joined the Muslims, wrapped her head in elaborate cloths, and talked about Allah. Somehow during that interminable fall and early winter of 1983, as she waited for word from the Court of Appeals, she began to think in the long term.

# CHAPTER 10

# STORIES

After Judge Barrett announced his decision in July 1982, Rebecca Allerton confided to me the rumor that the elusive Cynthia Shuford was Oscar Powell's girl friend; and as Marty Stolar worked on a brief for the appellate court during the fall and winter of 1982, I made some inquiries of my own in Binghamton. Some people said that Oscar Powell didn't have a girl friend. Some said he was homosexual. But others—three independent sources—said that Oscar Lee Powell did indeed have a girl friend named Cynthia Shubert or Shuffer or Shuford or something like that. My informants' estimates of how long they had been going together varied from "at least a few months" to "two or three years." When they told me that Shuford stayed with Oscar Lee in a housing project apartment rented to Margie Powell, I asked two friends to check on it for me. They had watched Shuford closely at the hearing and knew most of Bernadette Powell's family by sight; but unlike me, they wouldn't be recognized by the Powells. Before dawn one day they parked near the apartment in which Margie Powell said only she and Bernadette's son lived. A little after seven o'clock a young woman came out the front door, walked the few yards to the parking lot, and got into a waiting cab. She was wearing a heavy coat and dark sunglasses. It was Cynthia Shuford.

Some members of the Bernadette Powell Defense Fund

complained that Bernadette's family did little to help or support her, but the Powell family, it seemed, had ways of taking care of itself of which the defense-fund members never dreamed. How much did Bernadette Powell know about the "new evidence" and about the relationship between her brother and Cynthia Shuford? I asked her point-blank, and she seemed stunned. "Where'd you hear that? Girl friend, you say? I never did hear that." She thought her brother was gay, but she would ask him about it anyway, she said, and later she reported that the story wasn't true. Oscar said he scarcely knew Cynthia Shuford, though he had "seen her around," and once when he saw her in a club after she testified for Bernadette, he sent a drink over to her table. If she were needed to testify again, he was certain he wouldn't be able to find her.

There were other people I wanted to find. So, as Marty Stolar dickered with the appellate court, trying to get a hearing, I looked into a small factual matter that had bothered me for years. At Powell's trial, David Brown, describing the moment Al Smith entered Diane Nelson's apartment on the afternoon of June 26, 1978, named the other people who were present—Lisa Johnson (or Diaz), Diane Nelson, and "the other Diane Nelson." Lisa Johnson and Diane Nelson testified at the trial, but "the other Diane Nelson" did not appear. So, when *the* Diane Nelson mentioned in her testimony a day she spent "up to the other Diane's," courtroom spectators and several jurors hid their smiles. "The other Diane Nelson" seemed at that moment to be a figment of Diane Nelson's unreliable imagination, an alter ego, an imaginary friend.

But what if there really were another Diane Nelson? I wondered. What could she tell? I started looking for her, and soon, in response to a weak "Come in," I walked through a door in a public housing project in Ithaca and confronted a young woman who lay in bed, too painfully afflicted with arthritis to move. "I want to talk to you about Bernadette Powell," I said, expecting someone to eject me.

"I knew somebody would find me sooner or later," she said. "I'll try to get up. It would be a relief to talk about it." She shuffled slowly down the hall to the living room, her useless arms clutched to her sides, and settled herself gingerly on the edge of the couch. She explained that after her divorce a few years before she gave up the name Nelson to resume her family name, and that although she used her legal first name, Julia, on documents, she was always called by her second name, Diane. I had found the other Diane Nelson, and she wanted to talk.

Yes, she remembered very well that day in 1978 at Diane Nelson's apartment when Al Smith sold a gun to Bernadette Powell. Was it just before or just after Diane got out of the hospital after her bike accident? Anway, it must have been after school let out for the summer, because the boys were there playing together on the terrace—her own son and Diane's and Bernadette's. And it must have been sometime after three o'clock in the afternoon, because she never went out before that time. That afternoon she was sitting at Diane's dining table talking with Diane, who was cleaning up the kitchen. They were waiting for Diane's daughter to wake up from her nap, and then they were planning to go to the store. David Brown was there, standing in the doorway. Lisa Johnson came in, pushing her baby in a stroller, and sat down at the dining table. Julia, who knew Lisa only slightly, had heard from Diane that Lisa used a lot of drugs and often behaved strangely. Curious, Julia was so intent on observing Lisa, who seemed perfectly normal that day, that she didn't notice whether Bernadette Powell walked in with Al Smith or had been there in the back bedroom all along. She only caught a glimpse of Al Smith, who walked quickly down the hall to the bedroom without greeting anyone, but he must have been wearing his postal uniform, because she remembered the boys calling out from the terrace just before he walked in, "Here comes the mailman."

She grew up in the country with brothers who went hunting, so when she heard the gunshot from the back room she knew immediately what it was. The three boys rushed in from the terrace, and she herded them toward the door, yelling at Diane to get the baby out of the house. Al Smith ran past them out the door, and Bernadette followed. Everything was happening at once then. David Brown vanished and then appeared again saying something about a cap or a cap gun. Diane was screaming, "Goddammit, Bernadette! I told you not to bring no gun in this house!" When Bernadette left the house, Julia thought she might have been carrying a book. It seemed as though she left and then came back again. But by that time Julia was very upset. Of the moments after the gunshot she remembered little of what she saw but only her fear for the children and the sound of herself and of Diane yelling.

She remembered Bernadette's threats too, both before and after that day, though she heard them mostly secondhand through her best friend Diane. Even before Bernadette moved in with Diane she was sounding off about her ex-husband and all the terrible things he'd done to her. One day Diane took Julia up to Bernadette's apartment, just so Julia could see how beautiful it was. Bernadette possessed, as Diane put it, some "serious furniture," and she seemed to be a "serious cleaner" as well. The place was immaculate. That day they drank soda at a glass-topped table and talked about ways a woman could get even with a man, like pouring scalding water on him as he slept. But this conversation, Julia knew, was common to abused women like Bernadette and Diane. You didn't even have to be abused yourself to join in. It was enough to be a woman. So Julia didn't really take it seriously; and she knew that Bernadette also talked at times about how wonderful her ex-husband was. To Julia, Bernadette seemed to be a highly intelligent and ambitious woman, a hard worker, a concerned mother bent on getting ahead for herself and her boy. But she also seemed to be a confused woman, still in love and mixed up.

After she moved in with Diane, Bernadette's threats became more frequent and more specific. She began to rave about Herman in obscene language and to swear that she would shoot him. At least that's what Diane said, and after Bernadette moved into Diane's, Diane spent more and more time at Julia's nervously seeking advice about Bernadette. "She would tell Bernadette she wasn't going to listen anymore," Julia said, "but Bernadette wouldn't stop raving, so Diane would walk out and come up to my house and tell me about it. Diane kept saying, 'She's gonna do it.'"

After a time Julia grew worried, too, because she knew that Diane, despite all the difficulties of her life, was a good-humored, tolerant woman who usually could "snuff things off." But she couldn't snuff this off. Bernadette, Diane said, was even more serious about vengeance than she was about housekeeping. Bernadette made no secret of her plan. She talked of it to other people at Diane's apartment and even down at the Elks. "Everybody laughs about this wild woman," Diane told Julia. "Everybody sits her down and says, 'C'mon, Bernadette, tell us again how you're gonna off your old man.' Everybody thinks it's a joke, but I know she's really gonna do it." Julia suggested that Diane advise Bernadette to see a psychiatrist. Diane and Julia drove up in front of Diane's apartment one day in time to see Herman Smith run out the door followed, through the kitchen window, by Diane's new steam iron, which crashed into the headlight on Herman's parked car. "Let's get outta here," Diane said, watching her new iron bounce back onto the concrete walk. "That bitch is crazy." Driving away, leaving the iron on the sidewalk, Julia knew that Diane was scared. She recommended again that Diane tell Bernadette to see a therapist.

Julia offered to take me to visit her friend Diane Nelson. "She's had a very hard life," she said of Diane. "And most people think she's either pretty tough or pretty flaky, but she's really just another scared woman doing the best she can to make it on her own."

Distressed by the trial and its aftermath, Diane had moved to another city. People blamed her for "singing" about Bernadette, though she insisted she told the police nothing but what they told her she knew. Diane "seconded" the truth, Julia said, but she didn't volunteer it. Still, people harassed her. It got so she couldn't go into the Elks without somebody at the bar starting to sing a little song while others buried their laughter in their beer. Diane got upset when she had to give evidence at the preliminary hearing and Bernadette stood up and shouted at her because she'd told about Herman smoking dope in front of the child. Diane kept asking, "Whose side does Bernadette want me to be on anyway?" At first when she spoke to the police and the district attorney she tried to cover for Bernadette; at least she tried to make it sound as though Bernadette had good reason for doing what she did. But then, Julia said, Bernadette wrote a letter to Al Smith in which she called Diane a whore, and Al showed the letter to Diane, and Diane got upset all over again. Why would Bernadette say such things when Diane was doing her best to cover for her? She wept over it with Julia, who advised her to tell the simple truth.

"If you lie, you'll get in trouble," Julia said, "and you have three kids to look out for." It was for the sake of those kids, Julia said, that Diane spilled out more and more of her story.

"But why would Bernadette write to Al Smith?" I asked, as we drove to Diane Nelson's. "She said she didn't know him and she keeps on saying that."

"She knew him well enough to buy a gun from him," Julia said.

There they were again, the words I heard in court from Al Smith and Diane Nelson and David Brown and Joe Joch, the words I had not listened to. "Then what do you make of Bernadette?" I asked.

With one crippled hand Julia tugged her coat closer against the cold and offered a theory. "I didn't know her well, of course. Mostly just through what Diane told me about what she said and did. But I always thought she was a split personality."

That day just after Christmas when Julia and I dropped in on her unannounced, Diane Nelson was wearing a tight white knit minidress and black strappy shoes with very high heels. She had elaborate eyelashes and dangling bracelets and impossibly long fingernails brightly painted. Her hair was done up, coiled in a sophisticated chignon. She was dressed for what she would have called "some serious society," but she was busy cleaning the fish tank. She paced the living room waving a tiny net with which she skimmed the aquarium, snapping the flotsam onto the shag carpet. What with one courtroom and another, not to mention all the trouble she ran into at the Elks, she'd done about all the talking she wanted to do on the subject of Bernadette Powell. "You gotta understand," she said, "I lived off of subpoenas. Looks like everybody they picked up said, 'Go talk to Diane.' I'm saying, 'Oh no, don't go talk to Diane.' but that's what they did." But she dumped a pot of fresh water into the fish tank and sat down to tell her story again. "I know you're supposed to let the water get to be the same temperature and all, but any fish gonna live in my house is gonna have to learn how to deal." She took care to seem tough and savvy, but she couldn't explain why, when Bernadette moved into her apartment one day while Diane was out, it was Diane who wound up sleeping on the couch.

She told me, as Julia had, about the day Al Smith went back into Bernadette's bedroom and a gun went off. She too remembered shouting, "Goddammit, Bernadette." She explained that she had "specified to the max: Don't bring no gun into my house." So she was angry, but she wasn't surprised. Bernadette had been talking about shooting her ex-husband for so long, and Diane had been trying to talk her out of it. "You left him," Diane would remind Bernadette. "He didn't leave you. You didn't want him. Now leave the man alone." The trouble was, as far as Diane could see, nobody else much wanted Bernadette. "She'd get her a boyfriend—she especially liked the young guys—but after a while they'd find out how crazy she was and they'd split and leave her alone. She just got lonely. Then she wanted her old man back, only he didn't want getting back."

Diane didn't like seeing her new iron fly out the window. And she didn't like the way Bernadette talked about Herman in front of the children. "She was always talkin' up under the man's clothes, about what he was doing with them little white girls and all." That was no way to talk, Diane felt, in front of the man's child. Besides, Bernadette hadn't wanted the man; now she should let him mess with whoever he wanted to. She was messing around plenty herself, and what he did wasn't any of her business anymore. But it was the kerosene that did it, two big cans of kerosene Bernadette brought home and stored on the terrace. "I'm gonna burn him out," Bernadette said, and when Diane couldn't persuade her not to do it, she sneaked out on the terrace with a pail, poured out some kerosene, and replaced it with water.

It was just after that, she said, that she warned Al Smith. She knew he had a gun he'd been trying to get rid of, so she warned him, she said, for his sake and Bernadette's: "Don't you sell that woman no gun." Al Smith seemed to think that Bernadette needed a gun for protection, but Diane told him, "Bernadette don't need no protection, but somebody needs protection from Bernadette." Al Smith told Diane he wouldn't sell the gun to Bernadette, but then he went right ahead and did it anyway. Diane thought Al must have had "a thing" for Bernadette, must have thought that if he sold her the gun he could get close to her. After the gun went off that day in her apartment, they all tried to lie to Diane—Bernadette and David Brown and Lisa Johnson— all saying it was a cap. But she knew it was a gun, and Julia knew, and so did the cops who came traipsing in with their little search warrant fishing herb out of the ashtrays that morning Diane had such a hangover and was trying to get up to go to a wedding.

Once Bernadette had the gun, Diane was sure she'd use it. Half the time Bernadette talked about how she was going to make Herman pay. She would tell him that their son wanted them all to go camping together in Canada—he would do anything for the boy—and then she would shoot him and say it happened accidentally while they were fooling around with the gun. At other times, lonely times, Bernadette desperately wanted Herman back. Then she would talk about what a good husband he was. He hit her, Bernadette told Diane, only "one tiny time" after Bernadette hit the boy. Then Bernadette would pace up and down and keep asking Diane over and over, "Why won't he go back with me, Diane? Why won't he?"

"Do me a favor," Diane said, "and don't ask him, 'cause if you ask he might tell you something you don't want to hear, and then that man is a gone ass."

If Diane hadn't been so upset about Bernadette, she might have remembered to ask about the brakes before she got on the borrowed bike at the top of the steep hill running down from West Village to the Ithaca flats. An ambulance picked her up at the bottom and took her to the hospital; it was days before she got home again, and to be honest, she said, she didn't mind having a rest from Bernadette. But as soon as she got home that Sunday late in June Bernadette told her all about the pot party at Herman's the day before. The room was full of kids, she said, and Herman was in bed with some little white girl. Bernadette had gone down there to Endicott to drop off her son so Herman could take care of him for a couple of days, and that's what they walked in on. Herman knew they were coming, too. That's how he treated his son. Well, she'd get him this time, she said. She had read in the newspaper about a woman who shot her husband and got off with only one year. If she set it up right, she'd come out better than that. Anyway, she told Diane, she had been to see a psychiatrist and he couldn't help her. Now she was going to do things her way. Worn out, Diane said, "Bernadette, if it'll make you happy, go on and shoot the motherfucker."

The next afternoon Al Smith came over and the gun went

off in the back bedroom. Diane stopped speaking to Bernadette, and two days later Bernadette moved out, going to live in Owego. Enormously relieved, Diane tried to put the whole thing out of her mind. "I knew she was going to shoot him," she said, "but I didn't know how soon." Ten days later Herman Smith was dead.

"Don't get me wrong," Diane said to me, watching her fish twist lethargically in unexpected water. "I liked the girl. She could be very nice, very generous. But she was crazy."

"You mean hot-tempered, uncontrollable?"

"No—more like she was two different people," Diane replied. "She could be real nice and act very proper and everything, and then at other times it was like she had this Al Capone mind. She had a big thing for vengeance. You never knew if you did the least little thing to her what she might think of doing to you. Like one time some guy she was making it with hung up the phone on her 'cause he was trying to play poker; and she was gonna go shoot him. I said, 'C'mon, Bernadette, the man's just playing cards,' but I believe if she'd had a gun then she woulda shot him. And another time she had this guy staying in her apartment with her and she told him to get out, so he was getting out, and then she got mad that he was leaving and went after him with a butcher knife. It was my butcher knife, too."

"Remember that time the wheel fell off her car?" Julia prompted.

"Oh, yeah, and she was gonna find out who did it and blow them away. I said, 'Bernadette, what makes you think *somebody* did it? Couldn't the wheel just get loose and fall off?' No way. It had to be somebody out to get her. She was like paranoid. And then this Al Capone mind would take over and plan revenge. If they ever let her out of jail I'm gonna be long gone, because the first thing she's gonna do is come slipping up on Al and me."

Here was a Bernadette I had not met in the courtroom or on any of my visits—an angry, vengeful woman given to frequent indiscriminate sex and obscene language. But I

glimpsed her in the courtroom lavatory when I first introduced myself to Powell; I glimpsed her and put her out of
my mind. I heard of her again when I interviewed people
who had known Bernadette Powell before Herman's death.
Once in a black home in the Ithaca flats a young man who,
as a teenager in West Village, was friendly with Powell described her to me: educated, intelligent, articulate, ambitious, a good mother, a hard worker—all the qualities I
associated with the Bernadette Powell who was tried and
then befriended by the members of her defense committee
and the public. A woman who happened to be sitting in the
room finally broke in laughing: "Ya'll must be crazy as she
was. I knew Bernadette. She wasn't like that at all." Then
came the description of the angry, vengeful, sexy, and vulgar
woman I had heard of from others.

Because the descriptions of Bernadette Powell were as
contradictory as the testimony at the trial, she came to seem
more and more to me like a classic multiple personality.
Perhaps Julia's theory was correct. The contradictions of the
case seemed too immense to explain or to reconcile in any
other way. Someone had to be lying, yet all the people I
spoke to seemed to be telling the truth, at least as far as
they knew it. But what was "it"? Suppose there was not
one single truth but only many fragmentary and sometimes
contradictory truths? The trial had come down to a question
of who was lying: Al Smith, Diane Nelson, and the other
prosecution witnesses, or Bernadette Powell. But suppose
that none of them lied. Suppose there were two Berna-
dettes—an evil alter ego who plotted revenge and achieved
it, and the good one, the innocent one, who knew nothing
of these goings on, the one I arbitrarily chose to call the
"real" Bernadette. Perhaps the reason Bernadette Powell
could not remember buying a gun from Al Smith, when so
many other people did, was that the real Bernadette did not
buy the gun, but the false persona, the evil one, the one who
was angry and vengeful and vulgar did.

The only way I knew to test this theory was to talk with

Al Smith, but Al Smith wanted nothing to do with me. Like Diane Nelson, Al had "lived off of subpoenas." And from the minute he heard of Herman Smith's death and Bernadette Powell's arrest, Al Smith was terrified. Herman had been shot with *his* gun, he knew, and he was certain the cops would find him. He would lose his job, and then his wife and kids. He'd sat there on the couch in the back room at Ralph Brown's when the state cops came in nosing around, asking questions of everybody but him, and he knew they knew. He thought about killing himself, just to get it over with, but when he thought about being dead, with everything gone, the children gone, he couldn't stop crying. He'd sneak out in back of the post office and sit on the edge of the loading platform when none of the men were around and weep.

He'd given the money he got from Powell, the seventy-five dollars, to his wife, Sophie. He told her he won it in a card game at Ralph Brown's. (It was her uncle who gave him the gun in the first place—though he testified it was his brother-in-law—when they were still living in Brooklyn and he was working on the mail trucks. After a couple of men on a truck were shot during a mail robbery in Manhattan, Al decided he needed to carry a gun, and Sophie's uncle sent him one. When they cleared out of the city and went upstate, where the kids could have a better life, he took the gun along.) But after Bernadette Powell was arrested, he had to tell Sophie how he really got the money. He must go to the police and tell the truth, she insisted, and at last he agreed, but before he got around to it the police came to him.

He'd been through it then with the cops and Joe Joch— endless questions, endless subpoenas. He'd stayed away from the Elks, knowing what a hard time he'd get for cooperating with the honky D.A. to keep his white-ass job at the post office. But even on his mail route, up East Hill in a fairly fancy part of town, people would come to the door when he was dropping the mail in the box, to ask if he was Al Smith *the* mailman. Everything came out in the paper—how he had so many girl friends and beat up on some of them and once broke his wife's nose. (He hadn't known he broke it. He just took one swing and left the house, and it was a long time before he knew he'd left her with a broken nose.) What were his kids supposed to think?

Anyway, he'd done what he had to do—told the truth to the cops and given his testimony, and taken all the grief at the Elks, and somehow managed to keep his job. He'd quit drinking. He'd made some promises to Sophie and was trying harder this time. He never wanted to think about Bernadette Powell again. So when I called and asked him to meet me, I heard him catch his breath at the other end of the phone. Was he never going to be able to outlive the consequences of his act?

Like Diane Nelson he felt himself much maligned. Selling the gun was technically illegal, he knew, but he had tried to sell it to a "safe" person. He hadn't meant to do anything really *wrong*, he said. Yet he had somehow become a party to great wrongdoing, accountable in some inexplicable way for the death of another man who bore the same family name as himself. His guilt and his urge to vindicate himself overshadowed the troubles he'd been through. He told me the story about selling his gun to Powell, just as he told it at the trial, just as Diane and Lisa and David and Julia said it happened.

"But why did you do it?" I asked.

"I thought she was okay," he said. "I wanted for years to get rid of the gun—it was useless to me—but I had to make sure I was selling it to a safe person. I couldn't afford to have some dude buy my gun and turn around and commit an armed robbery."

"So how could you sell it to a woman who was swearing to kill her ex-husband?" I asked, picturing the vengeful Bernadette, the "unreal" Bernadette.

"But she wasn't. I didn't know her very well—only saw her a few times—but the reason I liked Bernadette is she was so different. She wasn't like those other deadbeat women up in West Village, just collecting their checks from week to week. She was really trying to get ahead. She went to school. She had a good job. She was doing everything she could for her son." (He was describing a woman like his wife.) "Some of those women up there were okay for a good time, but Bernadette you could really respect."

"But what did you think she was going to do with the gun?"

"She said she needed protection. She'd got this camper truck and she was planning on taking her son on trips. And she was buying a house down near where she worked. It was sort of out in the country, the way she described it, and she was going to be living there all by herself—with her son, I mean, but nobody else. So she needed protection."

"Didn't she tell you about her ex-husband, and how she wanted to get rid of him?"

"Bernadette? No way. She just wanted to get her life together."

"And didn't Diane Nelson ever warn you that it wouldn't be smart to sell a gun to Bernadette? Didn't Diane ever tell you that Bernadette was threatening to kill her ex-husband?"

"No," he said. "Never." He was headed out the door, making an excuse for a sudden errand. "If I'd known *that* do you think I would've sold it to her? The only reason I did is that I thought she was a hundred percent safe—the only person I could be sure wasn't ever going to use it. But now this whole thing has just about wrecked my life."

Al Smith hurried out, and my convenient split-personality theory fled with him. Al Smith, if I could believe him, sold the gun not to some vengeful, secret alter ego but to the sweet, industrious Bernadette, the "real" Bernadette. If Bernadette Powell was inhabited by two distinct personalities— that nice Miss Powell *and* Al Capone—they had worked toward a common goal.

I needed another theory, a reasonable story, something at last to tell myself to make it all come clear. I knew well enough what everyone said, on the record and off. I could even imagine their reasons for saying what they did. Take this question: Did Diane Nelson warn Al Smith not to sell a gun to Powell, as she said, or didn't she, as he said? Both felt guilty about Herman's death. Diane, knowing she should have warned Al, would come to believe that she had. And Al, knowing he should have heeded such a warning if she gave it, would come to believe that she had not. Everyone meant well enough, but compelled to put the best face on his or her own behavior, everyone rewrote the story to be its hero. Once you understood that, you could make sense of anyone's account. But when you thought about all the accounts at once, you couldn't square them up. You came no closer to the "truth."

A few days later I sat in the black Elks Club, under a row of photos of past benevolent and protective officers, drinking beer with the social director, Ralph Brown, proprietor of Ithaca's oldest floating poker game. "Sure Al and Bernadette knew each other," Brown said. "I've seen them talking together in my own living room. Most everybody at one time or another used to show up at my house." Was Bernadette sweet and upright, or was she gunning for her ex-husband? Both, Brown said. She'd been good to Brown, given him her old car when she got the new truck, just out of friendship. (Of course, after she shot Herman, Brown had a tough time explaining the car to the police, but she could be *that* generous.) On the other hand, he never would have sold her a gun. He would have told Al Smith not to do it, too, if only he'd known about it. But Al Smith never did mention it to him, at least not until after Herman was dead. Brown heard her threats. He liked Bernadette, even had a kind of crush on her, but he knew she could be serious trouble.

"You know, Brown," I said, "none of these stories really match up. Everybody's got a little bit different take on things, and I don't know who's lying. I don't even know if anybody *is* lying. I can't figure anything out anymore."

Brown offered me a sympathetic look and another beer. "Well, here's another story for you," he said. "The morning she shot Herman, Bernadette called me up. Must have been just a minute after she did it. I was asleep, so it didn't really sink in, but I figured it out later from the time in the newspapers. She just called me up and said, kind of excited, 'Brown, Brown.' "

"Did you ever tell the cops or the D.A.?"

"No," he said, inspecting the past officers on the wall. "Never told about it."

"What else did she say?"

"Well, she was quiet for a time. Probably knew I was half asleep. And then she just said, 'Never mind.' Just 'Never mind.' And she hung up and I went back to sleep, and that was all there was to that. Probably it didn't mean a thing." He paused. "When you think about it, though, it's kind of funny."

On December 28, 1983, Associate Justice Bernard S. Meyer of the New York State Court of Appeals ruled that Bernadette Powell's appeal based on Cynthia Shuford's new evidence presented "no issue of law" to the court. Marty Stolar's application for leave to appeal the decision of the appellate division in the matter of *People* v. *Powell* was therefore denied. Bernadette Powell had exhausted her recourse in the courts of the state of New York, for the second time. District Attorney Bucko told the press that Meyer's ruling "appears to have ended efforts to keep Powell's case alive."

# AFTERWORD

When Powell was admitted to Bedford Hills Correctional Facility, she was examined by a psychiatrist from the New York State Department of Mental Health. He found her to be perfectly normal though somewhat frightened and recommended that she be given reassurance and tranquilizers. She refused the drugs, but even without them, the psychiatrist reported, she was making a "good adjustment" to prison.

To Powell the adjustment was hard and erratic. She felt claustrophobic and couldn't bear to be locked up in her cell. She stood looking out through the tiny square of glass. For weeks she lost her speech, and when it returned it was unfamiliar, overlaid with a Puerto Rican accent. It took a long time to find again one voice she recognized, the educated polysyllabic lady, and another, the foxy street-wise woman. She switched back and forth like a bilingual traveler in foreign lands. In one voice she wrote tidy letters on pretty stationery, effusively thanking and blessing her defenders for their support. In another voice she dispatched imperious lists of things she needed: high boots with three-inch heels, a winter coat, hooded sweaters, blouses (silk or satin), pantyhose.

Sometimes she raged. Angrily she explained why so many people had lied about her. Al Smith, she said, was having an affair with Diane Nelson. Diane Nelson was having an affair with Herman. Diane wanted revenge on Bernadette because Bernadette reported her to the social services department as an unfit mother. Diane wanted revenge because Bernadette's baby-sitter was sleeping with Diane's boy-friend. David Brown wanted revenge because Bernadette would not take him as a lover. Lisa Johnson wanted revenge because Bernadette asked her to leave the house after seeing her strike the boy. Lisa Johnson wanted revenge because Bernadette would not take her as a lover. All of them were deeply envious of Bernadette because she was so clearly superior to them, pulling herself out of the housing project to buy a home of her own. And in any case, some of them, who so cleverly pretended to be her friends, were secretly the friends of Herman Smith. All of them were in conspiracy against her. Sometimes she thought about how to get even.

At first she prayed more than she ever had in her life, trying to keep her mind "detached" from prison. She signed up for prison college classes, thinking the initiative would count in her favor, and she did well; but by the time she received her associate's degree, she thought of school only as "the best escape" she knew from day-to-day life inside. Mostly she slept. She could fall asleep where she sat, without a moment's notice, and sleep for a few minutes or a few hours. And once asleep she could sleep through anything. The habit got her in trouble more than once when guards, thinking they had awakened her for some duty, found her later still asleep. They would write her up for disobeying an order she had slept through. "I sleep," she explained, "in a tight place." The other inmates nicknamed her "Sleeper" and "Ghost."

She worried about how her mind worked, or didn't work. Her memory was full of holes. Her prison experience seemed riddled with vacancy, as though someone had fired a shotgun through the fabric of her daily life. "It is becoming embarrassing to me," she wrote to Rebecca Allerton. "Such menial things I should remember just don't surface when I wish them to, or when I'm asked to recall something from a fellow inmate and end up faking it by saying, 'Oh yes, now I remember,' and really and truly do not remember." She feared she might be getting senile.

The holes in her history were more terrible. From the story of her past life, complete paragraphs fell away. Whole chapters vanished. Where did she live then? Did she go to school? Was she working? Where was Herman at that time? At the trial people said things about her and about Herman that she had put out of her mind. When Sanobia told about how Herman came in and hit Bernadette and kicked her down the stairs, it crossed her mind again, like a thin shadow of the event, too fleeting for memory. And the things Guydell and Oscar Lee said about the fights with Herman—she didn't remember much of that at all, though when they said it she knew it must be true. Whole pieces of her life seemed to be missing. She couldn't even remember getting married. When did it happen? Where? She couldn't remember what she was wearing, or Herman either, but she knew they must have looked nice.

"When I experience anxiety," she wrote, after taking some psychology courses in prison, "I find I forget things, or recall and repeat things I said previously." She came to understand why she lost some events, but she didn't know how many she lost or where they went. All her life, by forgetting, she shed bits and pieces of herself, and when she turned and looked for them, they were gone. Had she found them again, like small stones strewn along the way, they might have marked the trail back home. Instead, she was alone without a path.

She wanted me to find her. When I asked her questions about her past, she said over and over, "I don't remember. I don't know." But sometimes, when we had talked for hours and her resistance ran down, she would suddenly catch sight of something she had put out of her mind for years. She would scramble excitedly after it, and sometimes she would catch it before it rolled away again. Invariably the memory was something "bad"—a school failure, an abortion, the child given away. Twice she gave me letters she received from former lovers she could not remember. She wanted me to put the pieces together, to connect the dots and give her an outline, a shape visible to herself. She yearned to have the shape of innocence, but more than that she wanted to be whole.

I asked a psychiatrist experienced in criminal cases to visit Powell at Bedford Hills, and he returned from the interview looking downcast and speaking of dissociative thinking, blocking out, denial, poor object relations, defective reality testing, poor impulse control. He wanted to do some psychological testing and another prolonged interview before he wrapped up the symptoms and attached a diagnostic label to the whole package. But using only his preliminary findings he could argue that Powell, when she shot Herman Smith, acted in the grip of an "extreme emotional disturbance" or perhaps even legal insanity, and that when she went on trial she was unable to assist her attorney in her defense, unable to act reasonably in her own interests, unable at times even to be present. "I just felt helpless," she said, "and then people would be talking and I just saw their lips. I didn't hear what was being said. Sometimes that same thing would occur when I took the stand. . . . Sometimes I would answer yes or no in the wrong spot, not really comprehending what [the district attorney] was saying." Here, should anyone care to take it up, was the argument for a new appeal. Powell's trial could hardly be considered fair if she was, in some profound way, not *there*. The very fact that she stuck to her story, even after witnesses came forward to contradict her, the psychiatrist said, indicated her disturbance. A healthier person caught out in a deliberate lie would modify it, but Powell stuck to her story because in her mind it was the truth. A healthier person who killed with intent would accept her attorney's advice to plead guilty to manslaughter and settle for a short sentence, but Powell held out because in her mind she was innocent.

Probably few of the witnesses in the Powell case deliberately lied, though many of them, including the police experts, stretched a point. But none of them had the "truth" either. Our adversarial system of justice, a vestige of distant times and simpler beliefs, stages a contest between the truth and falsehood, good and evil, God and the devil. It never has been able to make allowances for the complexity we now see to be the human condition. If in the case of Bernadette Powell the courts unjustly convicted a disturbed woman, the alternative—to acquit her because she was disturbed—would have been unjust to Herman Smith. To the life of Bernadette Powell, to the life and death of Herman Smith, the courts were not so much unjust as immaterial. The process of trial and appeal and appeal again was an arduous exercise in irrelevancy, which became for Bernadette Powell "just part of the punishment."

If Powell's defenders were too quick to see her innocence, her prosecutors were too quick to see her guilt. It occurred to no one that she might have "troubles." Dirk Galbraith, at first satisfied with his "attractive client," never checked the basic facts of her story, and even when she clung unreasonably to her tale, contradicting prosecution and defense witnesses alike, he could see nothing but that she must be lying. He never thought of requesting a psychological evaluation of his client, for the legal defenses of extreme emotional disturbance and temporary insanity are reserved by legal tradition and mendacity for the rich and the white. Wealthy white people may suffer a disturbance (Jean Harris would appeal her conviction on these grounds), but poor black people just lie.

In the Powell case, prison too seems irrelevant. Confining Powell behind bars for fifteen years or more does not deter other people from committing similar crimes, for emotionally troubled people cannot reasonably assess the consequences of their actions and control themselves accordingly. It does not protect others from Powell, for the chances are remote that she would once again be caught in the particular configuration of desperate circumstances that provoked extreme violence. It does not rehabilitate Powell. Mistaken about where and how Powell went astray, prison cannot set her straight. And it does not punish her. Her suffering only confirms her profound sense of persecution, for she does not believe she did the act of intentional, premeditated murder for which she is imprisoned. And she knows, as everyone does, that many people who kill intentionally and far more brutally serve much shorter prison terms. (Of all those convicted of murder in the United States these days, two-thirds serve less than seven years, one-half less than four.) "I know I killed a man," she says, "and even though I never planned to do it, I'm willing to pay for it. But do I have to pay with my whole life? Isn't this too much?"

What is to be done for Bernadette Powell? Already more has been done for her by her defense committee, her lawyers, her sympathizers all across the country than is done for most convicted criminals, and it has only increased her suffering, raising her hopes and smashing them again. Often Powell says that if she had received earlier in life the love and concern the defense-committee members have shown her, her life would have been different. That is almost certainly true. But that is not the way it happened.

What is to be done about our courts and our prisons and our rising cry for capital punishment? Surely, through a great effort of imagination, this "system" might be refashioned closer to what we know of human life and what we dream of justice. But how? And who's to do it? How even to begin? The system as it is affords one remarkable convenience: most mistakes, under the press of new business, pass unnoticed. Surely it is easier not to remake the system but simply to erase the occasional mistake that comes to public attention.

In Texas Lenell Geter, alleged chicken-shack robber, was freed. Rather than speak of the injustice of his life sentence, we may now praise the justice that freed an innocent man after only a year in prison. In Ithaca, New York, the case of Bernadette Powell is already being erased. When I last spoke about the case at Cornell Law School in March 1984, the local radio station reported that I talked about the case of "Burnett" Powell who "murdered a man" in 1974 in Oswego, another town eighty miles up the road. The Cornell *Sun* reported that her "16-year-old son" was present at the killing.

Inside Bedford Hills Correctional Facility Bernadette Powell struggles against the seduction of hopelessness, the temptation to erase herself. In seasons of despair, she forgets to go to her classes. She forgets to eat. She wraps her head in her Muslim cloths and sits quietly. She sleeps. When I went to visit her in March she was angry with a visiting room guard, angry with Marty Stolar, angry with the defense committee, angry with me. The guard had made her leave her sweater in the anteroom. Marty Stolar "never did a damn thing" for her. The defense committee—down to five hard-core members—could no longer afford to send her monthly commissary money. And I had gotten her out of bed in the middle of the afternoon. "What do you have to come here for anyway?" she demanded. "And Ann Cedarholm too. She's still coming here every weekend. What for? When I get a visitor they make me get up and get dressed and come all the way down here, and when I come out of my cell I have to deal with all them women. What good does it do? Ain't nothing to do now but stay in my cell and sleep. When I can sleep I'm cool. It's all these damn visitors coming at all hours that get to me. So don't come no more. Unless you're coming to get me out of this place, don't come no more."

The next day she wrote a cheerful letter to thank me for my visit, saying how much she always enjoyed seeing me. She described her interesting new job as clerk in the prison library and her work on the student advisory committee for the college program. Her own courses were going well, she said (she was in fact keeping up a 3.6 grade-point average and twice had made the Dean's List), and at this rate she would get her bachelor's degree in behavioral sciences in

1985. She planned a break from classes during the summer, though, to prepare herself "mentally and spiritually" for the Muslim holy period of Ramadan, to which she looked forward with eagerness and great seriousness.

Of her troubles she wrote little—only that her son's school grades, which always had been excellent, had suddenly plummeted. "If only I knew my son's future was secure," she wrote, "I would gladly do this time standing on my head." (The child was always her greatest worry; her greatest punishment lay in knowing that when she was released from prison, he would be an adult, a man shaped by others.) She ended the letter, "I find that no matter how much things seem bad something in my nature compels me to keep hope that everything will turn out O.K. I think people tend to hold on to this feeling up to the last second."